MUCH ADO
ABOUT NOTHING

William Shakespeare

Prestwick House
LITERARY TOUCHSTONE CLASSICS
P.O. Box 658 Clayton, Delaware 19938 • www.prestwickhouse.com

SENIOR EDITOR: Paul Moliken

EDITOR: Elizabeth Osborne

DESIGN: Larry Knox

PRODUCTION: Jerry Clark

Prestwick House

P.O. BOX 658 • CLAYTON, DELAWARE 19938
TEL: 1.800.932.4593
FAX: 1.888.718.9333
WEB: www.prestwickhouse.com

Prestwick House Teaching Units™, Activity Packs™, and Response Journals™ are the perfect complement for these editions. To purchase teaching resources for this book, visit www.prestwickhouse.com

ISBN 978-1-58049-398-7

CONTENTS

STRATEGIES

STRATEGIES

Strategies for Understanding Shakespeare's Language

1. **When reading verse, note the appropriate phrasing and intonation.**

   DO NOT PAUSE AT THE END OF A LINE unless there is a mark of punctuation. Shakespearean verse has a rhythm of its own, and once a reader gets used to it, the rhythm becomes very natural to speak in and read. Beginning readers often find it helpful to read a short pause at a comma and a long pause for a period, colon, semicolon, dash, or question mark.

   Here's an example from *The Merchant of Venice*, Act IV, Scene i:

   > The quality of mercy is not strain'd, *(short pause)*
   > It droppeth as the gentle rain from heaven
   > Upon the place beneath: *(long pause)* it is twice blest; *(long pause)*
   > It blesseth him that gives, *(short pause)* and him that takes; *(long pause)*
   > 'Tis mightiest in the mighties; *(long pause)* it becomes
   > The throned monarch better than his crown; *(long pause)*

2. **Read from punctuation mark to punctuation mark for meaning.**

   In addition to helping you read aloud, punctuation marks define units of thought. Try to understand each unit as you read, keeping in mind that periods, colons, semicolons, and question marks signal the end of a thought. Here's an example from *The Taming of the Shrew*: Act I, Scene i:

   > Luc. Tranio, I saw her coral lips to move,
   >   And with her breath she did perfume the air;
   >   Sacred, and sweet, was all I saw in her.
   > Tra. Nay, then, 'tis time to stir him from his
   >   trance.
   >   I pray, awake, sir: if you love the maid,
   >   Bend thoughts and wits to achieve her.

The first unit of thought is from "Tranio" to "air":
He saw her lips move, and her breath perfumed the air.

The second thought ("Sacred, and sweet…") re-emphasizes the first.

Tranio replies that Lucentio needs to awaken from his trance and try to win "the maid." These two sentences can be considered one unit of thought.

3.   In an **inverted sentence**, the verb comes before the subject. Some lines will be easier to understand if you put the subject first and reword the sentence. For example, look at the line below:

"*Never was seen so black a day as this:*" (*Romeo and Juliet,* Act IV, Scene v)

You can change its inverted pattern so it is more easily understood:

"*A day as black as this was never seen:*"

4.   An **ellipsis** occurs when a word or phrase is left out. In *Romeo and Juliet,* Benvolio asks Romeo's father and mother if they know the problem that is bothering their son. Romeo's father answers:

"*I neither know it nor can learn of him*" (*Romeo and Juliet,* Act I, Scene i)

This sentence can easily be understood to mean,

"*I neither know [the cause of] it,
nor can [I] learn [about it from] him.*"

5.   As you read longer speeches, keep track of the subject, verb, and object— *who* did *what* to *whom.*

In the clauses below, note the subject, verbs, and objects:

Ross: The king hath happily received, Macbeth,
    The news of thy success: and when he reads
    Thy personal venture in the rebel's fight… (*Macbeth,* Act I, Scene iii)

1ˢᵗ clause: *The king hath happily received, Macbeth,/The news of thy success:*
SUBJECT – The king
VERB – has received

OBJECT – the news [of Macbeth's success]

2nd clause: *and when he reads/thy personal venture in the rebel's fight,*
SUBJECT – he [the king]
VERB – reads
OBJECT – [about] your venture

In addition to following the subject, verb, and object of a clause, you also need to track pronoun references. In the following soliloquy, Romeo, who is madly in love with Juliet, secretly observes her as she steps out on her balcony. To help you keep track of the pronoun references, we've made margin notes. (Note that the feminine pronoun sometimes refers to Juliet, but sometimes does not.)

> But, soft! what light through yonder window breaks?
> It is the east, and Juliet is the sun!
> Arise, fair sun, and kill the envious moon,
> Who* is already sick and pale with grief,   *"Who" refers to the moon.*
> That thou her* maid* art more fair than she:*   *"thou her maid" refers*
>   *to Juliet, the sun.*
>   *"she" and "her" refer to the moon.*

In tracking the line of action in a passage, it is useful to identify the main thoughts that are being expressed and paraphrase them. Note the following passage in which Hamlet expresses his feelings about the death of his father and the remarriage of his mother:

> O God! a beast that wants discourse of reason
> Would have mourn'd longer—married with my uncle,
> My father's brother, but no more like my father
> Than I to Hercules. (*Hamlet*, Act I, Scene ii)

Paraphrasing the three main points, we find that Hamlet is saying:

- a mindless beast would have mourned the death of its mate longer than my mother did
- she married my uncle, my father's brother
- my uncle is not at all like my father

If you are having trouble understanding Shakespeare, the first rule is to read it out loud, just as an actor rehearsing would have to do. That will help you understand how one thought is connected to another.

6. Shakespeare frequently uses **metaphor** to illustrate an idea in a unique way. Pay careful attention to the two dissimilar objects or ideas being compared. In *Macbeth*, Duncan, the king says:

> I have begun to plant thee, and will labour
> To make thee full of growing. (*Macbeth*, Act I, Scene v)

The king compares Macbeth to a tree he can plant and watch grow.

7. An **allusion** is a reference to some event, person, place, or artistic work, not directly explained or discussed by the writer; it relies on the reader's familiarity with the item referred to. Allusion is a quick way of conveying information or presenting an image. In the following lines, Romeo alludes to Diana, goddess of the hunt and of chastity, and to Cupid's arrow (love).

> ROMEO: Well, in that hit you miss: she'll not be hit
> with Cupid's arrow, she hath Dian's wit;
> and in strong proof of chastity well arm'd
> (*Romeo and Juliet*, Act I, Scene i)

8. Contracted words are words in which a letter has been left out. Some that frequently appear:

be't	on't	wi'	do't
t'	'sblood	'gainst	ta'en
i'	'tis	e'en	'twill
'bout	know'st	o'	ne'er
o'er			

9. Archaic, obsolete, and familiar words with unfamiliar definitions may also cause problems.

- **Archaic Words:** Some archaic words, like *thee, thou, thy,* and *thine,* are instantly understandable, while others, like *betwixt,* cause a momentary pause.

- **Obsolete Words:** If it were not for the notes in a Shakespeare text, obsolete words could be a problem; words like *beteem* are usually not found in student dictionaries. In these situations, however, a quick glance at the book's notes will solve the problem.

- **Familiar Words with Unfamiliar Definitions:** Another problem is those familiar words whose definitions have changed. Because readers think they know the word, they do not check the notes. For example, in this comment from *Much Ado About Nothing,* Act I, Scene i, the word *an* means "if":

> BEATRICE: Scratching could not make it worse, *an* 'twere such
> a face as yours were.

For this kind of word, we have included margin notes.

10. **Wordplay—puns, double entendres, and malapropisms:**

- A **pun** is a literary device that achieves humor or emphasis by playing on ambiguities. Two distinct meanings are suggested either by the same word or by two similar-sounding words.

- A **double entendre** is a kind of pun in which a word or phrase has a second, usually sexual, meaning.

- A **malapropism** occurs when a character mistakenly uses a word that he or she has confused with another word. In *Romeo and Juliet,* the Nurse tells Romeo that she needs to have a "confidence" with him, when she should have said "conference." Mockingly, Benvolio then says she probably will "indite" (rather than "invite") Romeo to dinner.

Reading Pointers for Sharper Insights

Consider the following as you read *Much Ado About Nothing*:

Characterization:

Beatrice and Benedick are two of the most complex, fully developed characters in all of Shakespeare's plays. Their complexity stems from their self-awareness; in the midst of mocking their friends and each other, they recognize their own faults.

The play itself is complex because we are given multiple views of these characters. We see Beatrice and Benedick through each other's eyes, and each through his or her own eyes. We also see them interacting with their friends and families; and we hear these friends and family members talk about them when they are absent.

- Benedick is aware of his own tendency to overstate the case—that his babbling, even when he is alone, is slightly self-mocking and intentional.

  He likes being part of the "fraternity" of men that includes Claudio and Pedro and feels comfortable enough to mock his friends, even when they do not seem to appreciate it. However, when the seriousness of the situation with Hero becomes apparent, it is Benedick who remains both reasonable and loyal.

- Beatrice says of herself, "I was born to speak all mirth and no matter." Other characters also comment on her natural cheerfulness, and so we can assume that, even when she is mocking Benedick, it is in a good-natured, rather than bitter, way.

  When, in Act III, Scene I, she hears herself criticized for being too sarcastic, notice how ready Beatrice is to let down her defenses and admit her own wrongdoing.

  She, like Benedick, is vulnerable and combative at the same time.

  Though they discount one another's opinion, Beatrice and Benedick are defined, even in their own eyes, by each other.

Language:

Also look out for uses and abuses of formal language. While Benedick and his friends seem to be well-born and educated and can, therefore, make complicated rhetorical jokes and allusions with ease, Dogberry and Verges fail utterly in their attempts to use elevated language.

MUCH ADO ABOUT NOTHING

WILLIAM SHAKESPEARE

DRAMATIS PERSONAE

DON PEDRO, Prince of Arragon
LEONATO, Governor of Messina
ANTONIO, an old man, brother of Leonato

BENEDICK, a young lord of Padua
BEATRICE, niece to Leonato
CLAUDIO, a young lord of Florence
HERO, daughter to Leonato
MARGARET, gentlewoman attending to Hero
URSULA, gentlewoman attending to Hero

DON JOHN, Don Pedro's bastard brother
BORACHIO, follower of Don John
CONRADE, follower of Don John

DOGBERRY, a Constable
VERGES, a Headborough
A Sexton
FIRST WATCHMAN
SECOND WATCHMAN

BALTHASAR, attendant on Don Pedro
FRIAR FRANCIS
A Boy
Messenger to Leonato
Another Messenger

Attendants, Musicians of the Watch, Antonio's Son and other Kinsmen

ACT I

SCENE I
[Before Leonato's House]

Enter Leonato, Governor of Messins; Hero, his daughter; and Beatrice, his niece, with a messenger.

LEONATO: I learn in this letter that Don Pedro of Arragon comes this night to Messina.

MESSENGER: He is very near by this. He was not three leagues off when I left him.

5　LEONATO: How many gentlemen have you lost in this action?

MESSENGER: But few of any sort, and none of name.

LEONATO: A victory is twice itself when the achiever brings home full numbers. I find here that Don Pedro hath bestowed much honour on a young Florentine called Claudio.

10　MESSENGER: Much deserved on his part, and equally remembered by Don Pedro. He hath borne himself beyond the promise of his age, doing in the figure of a lamb the feats of a lion. He hath indeed better bettered expectation than you must expect of me to tell you how.

15　LEONATO: He hath an uncle here in Messina who will be very much glad of it.

MESSENGER: I have already delivered him letters, and there appears much joy in him; even so much that joy could not show itself modest enough without a badge of bitterness.

20　LEONATO: Did he break out into tears?

MESSENGER: In great measure.

LEONATO: A kind overflow of kindness. There are no faces truer than those that are so washed. How much better is it to weep at joy than to joy at weeping!

25　BEATRICE: I pray you, is Signior Mountanto returned from the wars or no?

MESSENGER: I know none of that name, lady. There was none such in the army of any sort.

LEONATO: What is he that you ask for, niece?

HERO: My cousin means Signior Benedick of Padua.

30 MESSENGER: O, he's returned, and as pleasant as ever he was.

BEATRICE: He set up his bills here in Messina and challenged Cupid[1] at the flight; and my uncle's fool, reading the challenge, subscribed for Cupid and challenged him at the birdbolt.[2] I pray you, how many hath he killed and eaten

35   in these wars? But how many hath he killed? For, indeed I promised to eat all of his killing.[3]

LEONATO: Faith, niece, you tax Signior Benedick too much; but he'll be meet with you, I doubt it not.

MESSENGER: He hath done good service, lady, in these wars.

40 BEATRICE: You had musty[4] victual,[5] and he hath holp to eat it. He is a very valiant trencherman;[6] he hath an excellent stomach.

MESSENGER: And a good soldier too, lady.

BEATRICE: And a good soldier to a lady; but what is he to a

45   lord?

MESSENGER: A lord to a lord, a man to a man; stuffed with all honourable virtues.

BEATRICE: It is so indeed. He is no less than a stuffed man; but for the stuffing—well, we are all mortal.

50 LEONATO: You must not, my lord, mistake my niece. There is a kind of merry war betwixt Signior Benedick and her. They never meet but there's a skirmish of wit between them.

BEATRICE: Alas! He gets nothing by that. In our last conflict

55   four of his five wits went halting[7] off, and now is the whole man governed with one; so that if he have wit enough to keep himself warm, let him bear it for a difference between himself and his horse; for it is all the wealth that he hath left to be known a reasonable creature. Who

60   is his companion now? He hath every month a new sworn brother.

MESSENGER: Is't possible?

BEATRICE: Very easily possible. He wears his faith but as the fashion of his hat; it ever changes with the next block.

65 MESSENGER: I see, lady, the gentleman is not in your books.[8]

BEATRICE: No, and if he were, I would burn my study. But I pray you, who is his companion? Is there no young squarer now that will make a voyage with him to the devil?

---

[1] the god of love

[2] the novice level of archery (see glossary)

[3] [Beatrice implies that Benedick is a harmless soldier.]

[4] stale

[5] food

[6] good eater

[7] limping

[8] book of friends

70 MESSENGER: He is most in the company of the right noble
　　　Claudio.

BEATRICE: O Lord, he will hang upon him like a disease! He is
　　　sooner caught than the pestilence, and the taker runs pres-
　　　ently mad. God help the noble Claudio! If he have caught
75　　the Benedick, it will cost him a thousand pound ere he be
　　　cured.

MESSENGER: I will hold friends with you, lady.

BEATRICE: Do, good friend.

LEONATO: You will never run mad,[9] niece.

80 BEATRICE: No, not till a hot January.

MESSENGER: Don Pedro is approached.

*Enter Don Pedro, Claudio, Benedick, Balthasar, and [Don] John the
Bastard.*

DON PEDRO: Good Signior Leonato, are you come to meet your
　　　trouble? The fashion of the world is to avoid cost, and you
　　　encounter it.

LEONATO: Never came trouble to my house in the likeness of
85　　your Grace; for trouble being gone, comfort should remain;
　　　but when you depart from me, sorrow abides and happiness
　　　takes his leave.

DON PEDRO: You embrace your charge too willingly. I think this
　　　is your daughter.

90 LEONATO: Her mother hath many times told me so.

BENEDICK: Were you in doubt, my lord, that you asked her?

LEONATO: Signior Benedick, no; for then were you a child.

DON PEDRO: You have it full, Benedick. We may guess by this
　　　what you are, being a man. Truly, the lady fathers herself. Be
95　　happy, lady; for you are like an honourable father.

BENEDICK: If Signior Leonato be her father, she would not have
　　　his head on her shoulders for all Messina, as like him as she
　　　is.

BEATRICE: I wonder that you will still be talking, Signior Benedick;
100　Nobody marks you.

BENEDICK: What, my dear Lady Disdain! are you yet living?

BEATRICE: Is it possible Disdain should die while she hath such
　　　meet[10] food to feed it as Signior Benedick? Courtesy itself
　　　must convert to disdain if you come in her presence.

105 BENEDICK: Then is courtesy a turncoat. But it is certain I am loved
　　　of all ladies, only you excepted; and I would I could find in

[9] *[i.e., run mad with
the "plague" of
Benedick]*

[10] *suitable*

my heart that I had not a hard heart, for truly I love none.

BEATRICE: A dear happiness to women! They would else have
been troubled with a pernicious suitor. I thank God and
110   my cold blood, I am of your humour for that. I had rather
hear my dog bark at a crow than a man swear he loves
me.

BENEDICK: God keep your ladyship still in that mind! So some
gentleman or other shall scape a predestinate[11] scratched
115   face.

BEATRICE: Scratching could not make it worse an 'twere such
a face as yours were.

BENEDICK: Well, you are a rare parrot-teacher.

BEATRICE: A bird of my tongue is better than a beast of yours.

120 BENEDICK: I would my horse had the speed of your tongue, and
so good a continuer. But keep your way, a God's name!
I have done.

BEATRICE: You always end with a jade's[12] trick. I know you of
old.

125 DON PEDRO: That is the sum of all, Leonato. Signior Claudio
and Signior Benedick, my dear friend Leonato hath
invited you all. I tell him we shall stay here at the least a
month, and he heartily prays some occasion may detain
us longer. I dare swear he is no hypocrite, but prays from
130   his heart.

LEONATO: If you swear, my lord, you shall not be forsworn. [To
Don John] Let me bid you welcome, my lord. Being recon-
ciled to the prince your brother, I owe you all duty.

DON JOHN: I thank you. I am not of many words, but I thank
135   you.

LEONATO: Please it your Grace lead on?

DON PEDRO: Your hand, Leonato. We will go together.

Exeunt [all but] Benedick and Claudio.

CLAUDIO: Benedick, didst thou note the daughter of Signior
Leonato?

140 BENEDICK: I noted her not, but I looked on her.

CLAUDIO: Is she not a modest[13] young lady?

BENEDICK: Do you question me, as an honest man should do,
for my simple true judgment? or would you have me
speak after my custom, as being a professed tyrant to
145   their sex?

CLAUDIO: No. I pray thee speak in sober judgment.

BENEDICK: Why, i' faith, methinks she's too low for a high
praise, too brown for a fair praise, and too little for a great

[11]*fated*

[12]*worthless horse's*
[see glossary]

[13]*mild*

praise. Only this commendation I can afford her, that were
she other than she is, she were unhandsome, and being no
150   other but as she is, I do not like her.

CLAUDIO: Thou thinkest I am in sport. I pray thee tell me truly
how thou likest her.

BENEDICK: Would you buy her, that you enquire after her?

CLAUDIO: Can the world buy such a jewel?

155 BENEDICK: Yea, and a case to put it into. But speak you this with a
sad brow? or do you play the flouting Jack, to tell us Cupid
is a good hare-finder and Vulcan a rare carpenter?[14] Come,
in what key shall a man take you to go in the song?

CLAUDIO: In mine eye she is the sweetest lady that ever I looked
160   on.

BENEDICK: I can see yet without spectacles, and I see no such
matter. There's her cousin, an she were not possessed with a
fury, exceeds her as much in beauty as the first of May doth
the last of December. But I hope you have no intent to turn
165   husband, have you?

CLAUDIO: I would scarce trust myself, though I had sworn the
contrary, if Hero would be my wife.

BENEDICK: Is't come to this? In faith, hath not the world one man
but he will wear his cap with suspicion? Shall I never see a
170   bachelor of threescore again? Go to, i' faith! An thou wilt
needs thrust thy neck into a yoke, wear the print of it and
sigh away Sundays. Look; Don Pedro is returned to seek
you.

Enter Don Pedro.

DON PEDRO: What secret hath held you here, that you followed
175   not to Leonato's?

BENEDICK: I would your Grace would constrain me to tell.

DON PEDRO: I charge thee on thy allegiance.

BENEDICK: You hear, Count Claudio. I can be secret as a dumb
man, I would have you think so; but, on my allegiance—
180   mark you this—on my allegiance! he is in love. With who?
Now that is your Grace's part. Mark how short his answer
is: With Hero, Leonato's short daughter.

CLAUDIO: If this were so, so were it uttered.

BENEDICK: Like the old tale, my lord: 'it is not so, nor 'twas not so;
185   but indeed, God forbid it should be so!'[15]

CLAUDIO: If my passion change not shortly, God forbid it should
be otherwise.

[14] [*Benedick asks if Claudio is teasing; see glossary*]

[15] *refrain from a fairy tale*

DON PEDRO: Amen, if you love her; for the lady is very well
    worthy.

190 CLAUDIO: You speak this to fetch me in, my lord.

DON PEDRO: By my troth, I speak my thought.

CLAUDIO: And, in faith, my lord, I spoke mine.

BENEDICK: And, by my two faiths and troths, my lord, I spoke
    mine.

195 CLAUDIO: That I love her, I feel.

DON PEDRO: That she is worthy, I know.

BENEDICK: That I neither feel how she should be loved, nor
    know how she should be worthy, is the opinion that fire
    cannot melt out of me. I will die in it at the stake.

200 DON PEDRO: Thou wast ever an obstinate heretic in the despite
    of beauty.

CLAUDIO: And never could maintain his part but in the force
    of his will.

BENEDICK: That a woman conceived me, I thank her; that she
205   brought me up, I likewise give her most humble thanks;
    but that I will have a recheate[16] winded[17] in my forehead,
    or hang my bugle in an invisible baldrick,[18] all women
    shall pardon me. Because I will not do them the wrong
    to mistrust any, I will do myself the right to trust none;
210   and the fine is, for the which I may go the finer, I will
    live a bachelor.

DON PEDRO: I shall see thee, ere I die, look pale with love.

BENEDICK: With anger, with sickness, or with hunger, my lord;
    not with love. Prove that ever I lose more blood with love
215   than I will get again with drinking,[19] pick out mine eyes
    with a ballad-maker's pen and hang me up at the door of
    a brothel house for the sign of blind Cupid.

DON PEDRO: Well, if ever thou dost fall from this faith, thou
    wilt prove a notable argument.

220 BENEDICK: If I do, hang me in a bottle like a cat and shoot at
    me; and he that hits me, let him be clapped on the shoul-
    der and called Adam.[20]

DON PEDRO: Well, as time shall try. 'In time the savage bull
    doth bear the yoke.'[21]

225 BENEDICK: The savage bull may; but if ever the sensible
    Benedick bear it, pluck off the bull's horns and set them
    in my forehead, and let me be vilely painted, and in such
    great letters as they write 'Here is good horse to hire,' let
    them signify under my sign. 'Here you may see Benedick
230   the married man.'

[16]*hunting horn*

[17]*blown*

[18]*belt-strap*

[19][*Wine was thought to increase blood levels.*]

[20][*Adam Bell was a legendary archer.*]

[21][*an old proverb*]

CLAUDIO: If this should ever happen, thou wouldst be horn-mad.

DON PEDRO: Nay, if Cupid have not spent all his quiver in Venice, thou wilt quake for this shortly.

BENEDICK: I look for an earthquake too, then.

235 DON PEDRO: Well, you will temporize[22] with the hours. In the meantime, good Signior Benedick, repair to Leonato's, commend me to him and tell him I will not fail him at supper; for indeed he hath made great preparation.

BENEDICK: I have almost matter enough in me for such an embas-
240 sage;[23] and so I commit you—

CLAUDIO: To the tuition[24] of God. From my house—if I had it—

DON PEDRO: The sixth of July. Your loving friend, Benedick.

BENEDICK: Nay, mock not, mock not. The body of your discourse is sometime guarded with fragments, and the guards are but
245 slightly basted on neither.[25] Ere you flout old ends any further, examine your conscience. And so I leave you.   *[Exit.]*

CLAUDIO: My liege, your highness now may do me good.

DON PEDRO: My love is thine to teach. Teach it but how,
      And thou shalt see how apt it is to learn
250   Any hard lesson that may do thee good.

CLAUDIO: Hath Leonato any son, my lord?

DON PEDRO: No child but Hero; she's his only heir. Dost thou affect her, Claudio?

CLAUDIO: O my lord,
255   When you went onward on this ended action,
      I looked upon her with a soldier's eye,
      That liked, but had a rougher task in hand
      Than to drive liking to the name of love;
      But now I am returned and that war-thoughts
260   Have left their places vacant, in their rooms
      Come thronging soft and delicate desires,
      All prompting me how fair young Hero is,
      Saying I liked her ere I went to wars.

DON PEDRO: Thou wilt be like a lover presently
265   And tire the hearer with a book of words.
      If thou dost love fair Hero, cherish it,
      And I will break with her and with her father,
      And thou shalt have her. Wast not to this end
      That thou began'st to twist so fine a story?

270 CLAUDIO: How sweetly you do minister to love,
      That know love's grief by his complexion![26]
      But lest my liking might too sudden seem,
      I would have salved[27] it with a longer treatise.[28]

[22]*grow milder; also a pun on "temporize," meaning "make time"*

[23]*errand*

[24]*protection; Claudio and Don Pedro mockingly pick up on Benedick's "I commit you," which is a phrase often used to close letters.*

[25]*[Benedick retorts by criticizing his friends' style of speaking; see glossary]*

[26]*appearance*

[27]*amended*

[28]*explanation*

DON PEDRO: What need the bridge much broader than the
275   flood?
         The fairest grant is the necessity.
         Look, what will serve is fit.
         'Tis once, thou lovest,
         And I will fit thee with the remedy.
280   I know we shall have revelling to-night.
         I will assume thy part in some disguise
         And tell fair Hero I am Claudio,
         And in her bosom I'll unclasp my heart
         And take her hearing prisoner with the force
285   And strong encounter of my amorous tale.
         Then after to her father will I break;
         And the conclusion is, she shall be thine.
         In practice let us put it presently.   *Exeunt.*

SCENE II
[A Room in Leonato's House]

Enter Leonato and [Antonio] brother to Leonato.

LEONATO: How now, brother? Where is my cousin, your son?
         Hath he provided this music?
ANTONIO: He is very busy about it. But, brother, I can tell you
         strange news that you yet dreamt not of.
5   LEONATO: Are they good?
ANTONIO: As the event stamps them; but they have a good
         cover, they show well outward. The prince and Count
         Claudio, walking in a thick-pleached²⁹ alley in mine
         orchard, were thus much overheard by a man of mine;
10   the prince discovered to Claudio that he loved my niece
         your daughter and meant to acknowledge it this night in
         a dance, and if he found her accordant, he meant to take
         the present time by the top and instantly break with you
         of it.
15 LEONATO: Hath the fellow any wit that told you this?
ANTONIO: A good sharp fellow. I will send for him, and ques-
         tion him yourself.
LEONATO: No, no. We will hold it as a dream till it appear
         itself; but I will acquaint my daughter withal,³⁰ that she

²⁹*thick with hedges*

³⁰*with it*

20   may be the better prepared for an answer, if peradventure[31]
        this be true. Go you and tell her of it.

Enter musician.

        Cousin, you know what you have to do. —*[To the musician]*
        O, I cry you mercy, friend. Go you with me, and I will use
        your skill.—Good cousin, have a care this busy time.

                                                    [Exeunt.]

[31]*perhaps*

SCENE III
[Another Room in Leonato's House]

Enter Sir [Don] John and Conrade, his companion

CONRADE: What the goodyear, my lord! Why are you thus out of
        measure sad?
DON JOHN: There is no measure[32] in the occasion that breeds;[33]
        therefore the sadness is without limit.
5 CONRADE: You should hear reason.
DON JOHN: And when I have heard it, what blessings brings it?
CONRADE: If not a present remedy, at least a patient sufferance.
DON JOHN: I wonder that thou being, as thou say'st thou art, born
        under Saturn,[34] goest about to apply a moral medicine to a
10   mortifying mischief. I cannot hide what I am: I must be sad
        when I have cause, and smile at no man's jests; eat when I
        have stomach, and wait for no man's leisure; sleep when I
        am drowsy, and tend on no man's business; laugh when I am
        merry, and claw no man in his humour.
15 CONRADE: Yea, but you must not make the full show of this till
        you may do it without controlment. You have of late stood
        out against your brother, and he hath ta'en you newly into
        his grace, whereit is impossible you should take true root
        but by the fair weather that you make yourself. It is needful
20   that you frame the season for your own harvest.
DON JOHN: I had rather be a canker[35] in a hedge than a rose in his
        grace, and it better fits my blood to be disdained of all than
        to fashion a carriage to rob love from any. In this, though
        I cannot be said to be a flattering honest man, it must not
25   be denied but I am a plain-dealing villain. I am trusted with
        a muzzle and enfranchised[36] with a clog;[37] therefore I have

[32]*limit*

[33]*causes [my sad-
ness]*

[34]*[supposedly mak-
ing him gloomy;
see glossary]*

[35]*prickly, wild rose*

[36]*set free*

[37]*heavy piece of
wood; burden*

decreed not to sing in my cage. If I had my mouth, I would bite; if I had my liberty, I would do my liking. In the meantime let me be that I am, and seek not to alter

30   me.

CONRADE: Can you make no use of your discontent?

DON JOHN: I make all use of it, for I use it only.

Enter Borachio.

Who comes here? What news, Borachio?

BORACHIO: I came yonder from a great supper. The prince your

35   brother is royally entertained by Leonato, and I can give you intelligence of an intended marriage.

DON JOHN: Will it serve for any model to build mischief on? What is he for a fool that betroths himself to unquiet-ness?

40 BORACHIO: Marry, it is your brother's right hand.

DON JOHN: Who? the most exquisite Claudio?

BORACHIO: Even he.

DON JOHN: A proper squire! And who? and who? which way looks he?

45 BORACHIO: Marry, on Hero, the daughter and heir of Leonato.

DON JOHN: A very forward March-chick![38] How came you to this?

BORACHIO: Being entertained[39] for a perfumer, as I was smok-ing a musty room, comes me the prince and Claudio,

50   hand in hand in sad conference. I whipt me behind the arras and there heard it agreed upon that the prince should woo Hero for himself, and having obtained her, give her to Count Claudio.

DON JOHN: Come, come, let us thither. This may prove food to

55   my displeasure. That young start-up hath all the glory of my overthrow. If I can cross him any way, I bless myself every way. You are both sure, and will assist me?

CONRADE: To the death, my lord.

DON JOHN: Let us to the great supper. Their cheer is the

60   greater that I am subdued. Would the cook were of my mind! Shall we go prove what's to be done?

BORACHIO: We'll wait upon your lordship.

Exeunt.

[38]*i.e., a precocious child*

[39]*employed*

ACT II

SCENE I
[A Hall in Leonato's House]

Enter Leonato; his brother, [Antonio], Hero, his daughter; and Beatrice, his niece and a kinsman.

LEONATO: Was not Count Don John here at supper?

ANTONIO: I saw him not.

BEATRICE: How tartly¹ that gentleman looks! I never can see him but I am heart-burned an hour after.

5 HERO: He is of a very melancholy disposition.

BEATRICE: He were an excellent man that were made just in the midway between him and Benedick. The one is too like an image and says nothing, and the other too like my lady's eldest son, evermore tattling.

10 LEONATO: Then half Signior Benedick's tongue in Count Don John's mouth, and half Count Don John's melancholy in Signior Benedick's face—

BEATRICE: With a good leg and a good foot, uncle, and money enough in his purse, such a man would win any woman in

15 the world—if 'a could get her good will.

LEONATO: By my troth, niece, thou wilt never get thee a husband if thou be so shrewd of thy tongue.

ANTONIO: In faith, she's too curst.²

BEATRICE: Too curst is more than curst. I shall lessen God's send-

20 ing that way, for it is said, 'God sends a curst cow short horns';³ but to a cow too curst he sends none.

LEONATO: So, by being too curst, God will send you no horns.

BEATRICE: Just, if he send me no husband; for the which blessing I am at him upon my knees every morning and evening. Lord,

25 I could not endure a husband with a beard on his face. I had rather lie in the woollen!⁴

LEONATO: You may light on a husband that hath no beard.

¹*sourly*

²*sharp-tempered*

³*[a sexual pun]*

⁴*wool blankets*

23

BEATRICE: What should I do with him? dress him in my apparel and make him my waiting gentlewoman? He that hath a beard is more than a youth, and he that hath no beard is less than a man; and he that is more than a youth is not for me; and he that is less than a man, I am not for him. Therefore I will even take sixpence in earnest of the bear-ward and lead his apes into hell.[5]

35 LEONATO: Well then, go you into hell?

BEATRICE: No; but to the gate, and there will the devil meet me like an old cuckold with horns on his head, and say 'Get you to heaven, Beatrice, get you to heaven. Here's no place for you maids.' So deliver I up my apes, and away to Saint Peter—for the heavens. He shows me where the bachelors sit, and there live we as merry as the day is long.

ANTONIO: [To Hero] Well, niece, I trust you will be ruled by your father.

45 BEATRICE: Yes faith. It is my cousin's duty to make courtesy and say, 'Father, as it please you.' But yet for all that, cousin, let him be a handsome fellow, or else make another courtesy, and say, 'Father, as it please me.'

LEONATO: Well, niece, I hope to see you one day fitted with a husband.

BEATRICE: Not till God make men of some other metal than earth. Would it not grieve a woman to be overmastered with a piece of valiant dust? to make an account of her life to a clod of wayward marl?[6] No, uncle, I'll none. Adam's sons are my brethren, and truly I hold it a sin to match in my kindred.

LEONATO: Daughter, remember what I told you. If the prince do solicit you in that kind, you know your answer.

BEATRICE: The fault will be in the music, cousin, if you be not wooed in good time. If the prince be too important, tell him there is measure in everything, and so dance out the answer. For, hear me, Hero, wooing, wedding, and repenting is as a Scotch jig, a measure, and a cinque-pace:[7] the first suit is hot and hasty like a Scotch jig—and full as fantastical; the wedding, mannerly modest, as a measure, full of state and ancientry;[8] and then comes repentance and with his bad legs falls into the cinque-pace faster and faster, till he sink into his grave.

LEONATO: Cousin, you apprehend passing shrewdly.

---

[5] [Leading apes in hell was the proverbial punishment of old maids. Bear-trainers sometimes kept apes in addition to bears, so Beatrice says that she will accept payment from the bear-trainer to lead his apes.]

[6] clay

[7] five-step dance

[8] formality

70 BEATRICE: I have a good eye, uncle; I can see a church by day-
    light.
LEONATO: The revellers are entering, brother. Make good room.

Enter Prince [Don] Pedro, Claudio, Benedick, Balthasar, [Don]
John, [Borachio, Margaret, Ursula, and others, masked.]

DON PEDRO: Lady, will you walk about with your friend?
HERO: So you walk softly and look sweetly and say nothing, I am
75   yours for the walk; and especially when I walk away.
DON PEDRO: With me in your company?
HERO: I may say so when I please.
DON PEDRO: And when please you to say so?
HERO: When I like your favour,⁹ for God defend the lute should
80   be like the case!¹⁰
DON PEDRO: My visor is Philemon's¹¹ roof; within the house is
    Jove.
HERO: Why then, your visor should be thatched.¹²
DON PEDRO: Speak low if you speak love.   *[Draws her aside.]*
85 BALTHASAR: Well, I would you did like me.
MARGARET: So would not I for your own sake, for I have many
    ill qualities.
BALTHASAR: Which is one?
MARGARET: I say my prayers aloud.
90 BALTHASAR: I love you the better. The hearers may cry Amen.
MARGARET: God match me with a good dancer!
BALTHASAR: Amen.
MARGARET: And God keep him out of my sight when the dance is
    done! Answer, clerk.¹³
95 BALTHASAR: No more words. The clerk is answered.
                                        [Takes her aside.]
URSULA: I know you well enough. You are Signior Antonio.
ANTONIO: At a word, I am not.
URSULA: I know you by the waggling of your head.
ANTONIO: To tell you true, I counterfeit him.
100 URSULA: You could never do him so ill-well unless you were the
    very man. Here's his dry hand up and down. You are he,
    you are he!
ANTONIO: At a word, I am not.
URSULA: Come, come, do you think I do not know you by your
105   excellent wit? Can virtue hide itself? Go to, mum, you are
    he. Graces will appear, and there's an end.
                                        [They step aside.]

⁹*appearance*

¹⁰*i.e., that your*
face should be like
your mask

¹¹*[the elderly host*
of the god Jove;
see glossary]

¹²*woven*

¹³*[Margaret pre-*
tends Balthasar
is giving formal
answers during
a church service;
see glossary]

BEATRICE: Will you not tell me who told you so?

BENEDICK: No, you shall pardon me.

BEATRICE: Nor will you not tell me who you are?

110 BENEDICK: Not now.

BEATRICE: That I was disdainful, and that I had my good wit out of the Hundred Merry Tales[14]—well, this was Signior Benedick that said so.

BENEDICK: What's he?

115 BEATRICE: I am sure you know him well enough.

BENEDICK: Not I, believe me.

BEATRICE: Did he never make you laugh?

BENEDICK: I pray you, what is he?

BEATRICE: Why, he is the prince's jester, a very dull fool. Only
120   his gift is in devising impossible slanders. None but lib-
    ertines delight in him; and the commendation is not in
    his wit, but in his villainy; for he both pleases men and
    angers them, and then they laugh at him and beat him. I
    am sure he is in the fleet. I would he had boarded[15] me.

125 BENEDICK: When I know the gentleman, I'll tell him what you
    say.

BEATRICE: Do, do. He'll but break a comparison or two on
    me; which peradventure, not marked or not laughed at,
    strikes him into melancholy; and then there's a partridge
130   wing saved, for the fool will eat no supper that night. We
    must follow the leaders.

BENEDICK: In every good thing.

BEATRICE: Nay, if they lead to any ill, I will leave them at the
    next turning.   *Music for the dance.*

> *Exeunt. [All but Don John, Borachio, and Claudio.]*

135 DON JOHN: Sure my brother is amorous on Hero and hath
    withdrawn her father to break with him about it. The
    ladies follow her and but one visor remains.

BORACHIO: And that is Claudio. I know him by his bearing.

DON JOHN: Are you not Signior Benedick?

140 CLAUDIO: You know me well. I am he.

DON JOHN: Signior, you are very near my brother in his love.
    He is enamoured on Hero. I pray you dissuade him from
    her; she is no equal for his birth. You may do the part of
    an honest man in it.

145 CLAUDIO: How know you he loves her?

DON JOHN: I heard him swear his affection.

BORACHIO: So did I too, and he swore he would marry her
    tonight.

---

14 *a popular joke book*

15 *approached*

DON JOHN: Come, let us to the banquet.

Exeunt [Don John and Borachio.]

150 CLAUDIO: Thus answer I in name of Benedick,
But hear these ill news with the ears of Claudio.
'Tis certain so; the prince woos for himself.
Friendship is constant in all other things
Save in the office and affairs of love.
155 Therefore all hearts in love use their own tongues;
Let every eye negotiate for itself,
And trust no agent; for beauty is a witch
Against whose charms faith melteth into blood.
This is an accident[16] of hourly proof,[17]
160 Which I mistrusted not. Farewell therefore Hero!

Enter Benedick [unmasked.]

BENEDICK: Count Claudio?

CLAUDIO: Yea, the same.

BENEDICK: Come, will you go with me?

CLAUDIO: Whither?

165 BENEDICK: Even to the next willow,[18] about your own business,
county.[19] What fashion will you wear the garland of? about
your neck, like an usurer's chain? or under your arm, like a
lieutenant's scarf? You must wear it one way, for the prince
hath got your Hero.

170 CLAUDIO: I wish him joy of her.

BENEDICK: Why, that's spoken like an honest drovier.[20] So they
sell bullocks. But did you think the prince would have
served you thus?

CLAUDIO: I pray you leave me.

175 BENEDICK: Ho! now you strike like the blind man! 'Twas the boy
that stole your meat, and you'll beat the post.

CLAUDIO: If it will not be, I'll leave you.   *Exit.*

BENEDICK: Alas, poor hurt fowl! now will he creep into sedges.
But, that my Lady Beatrice should know me, and not know
180 me! The prince's fool! Ha! it may be I go under that title
because I am merry. Yea, but so I am apt to do myself wrong.
I am not so reputed. It is the base though bitter, disposition
of Beatrice that puts the world into her person and so gives
me out. Well, I'll be revenged as I may.

Enter [The Prince] Don Pedro.

[16]*instance*

[17]*i.e., proved over and over again*

[18]*[A willow garland symbolized lost love.]*

[19]*count*

[20]*cattle salesman*

185 Don Pedro: Now, signior, where's the count? Did you see
him?

Benedick: Troth, my lord, I have played the part of Lady
Fame. I found him here as melancholy as a lodge²¹ in a
warren. I told him, and I think I told him true, that your
190 grace had got the good will of this young lady, and I
offered him my company to a willow tree, either to make
him a garland, as being forsaken, or to bind him up a rod,
as being worthy to be whipped.

Don Pedro: To be whipped? What's his fault?

195 Benedick: The flat transgression of a schoolboy who, being
overjoyed with finding a bird's nest, shows it his companion, and he steals it.

Don Pedro: Wilt thou make a trust a transgression? The transgression is in the stealer.

200 Benedick: Yet it had not been amiss the rod²² had been made,
and the garland too; for the garland he might have worn
himself, and the rod he might have bestowed²³ on you,
who, as I take it, have stolen his birds' nest.

Don Pedro: I will but teach them to sing and restore them to
205 the owner.

Benedick: If their singing answer your saying, by my faith, you
say honestly.

Don Pedro: The Lady Beatrice hath a quarrel to you. The
gentleman that danced with her told her she is much
210 wronged by you.

Benedick: O, she misused me past the endurance of a block!
An oak but with one green leaf on it would have answered
her; my very visor began to assume life and scold with
her. She told me, not thinking I had been myself, that
215 I was the prince's jester, that I was duller than a great
thaw;²⁴ huddling jest upon jest with such impossible
conveyance upon me that I stood like a man at a mark,
with a whole army shooting at me. She speaks poniards,²⁵
and every word stabs. If her breath were as terrible as her
220 terminations, there were no living near her; she would
infect to the North Star. I would not marry her though
she were endowed with all that Adam had left him before
he transgressed. She would have made Hercules²⁶ have
turned spit, yea, and have cleft his club to make the fire
225 too. Come, talk not of her. You shall find her the infernal
Ate²⁷ in good apparel. I would to God some scholar would

²¹single occupant

²²whip

²³used

²⁴a day one is
trapped inside
because of melting
snow

²⁵daggers

²⁶strongest man
in the world; see
glossary

²⁷one of the
Furies—Greek
goddesses of
vengeance and
discord

conjure[28] her, for certainly, while she is here, a man may live
as quiet in hell as in a sanctuary; and people sin upon purpose, because they would go thither; so indeed all disquiet,
230   horror, and perturbation follows her.

Enter Claudio, Beatrice, Leonato, and Hero.

DON PEDRO: Look, here she comes.
BENEDICK: Will your Grace command me any service to the
world's end? I will go on the slightest errand now to the
Antipodes[29] that you can devise to send me on; I will fetch
235   you a toothpicker now from the furthest inch of Asia; bring
you the length of Prester Don John's[30] foot; fetch you a hair
off the great Cham's[31] beard; do you any embassage to the
Pygmies—rather than hold three words' conference with
this harpy.[32] You have no employment for me?
240 DON PEDRO: None, but to desire your good company.
BENEDICK: O God, my lord, here's a dish I love not! I cannot
endure my Lady Tongue.   *Exit.*
DON PEDRO: Come, lady, come; you have lost the heart of Signior
Benedick.
245 BEATRICE: Indeed, my lord, he lent it me awhile, and I gave him
use for it—a double heart for his single one. Marry, once
before he won it of me with false dice; therefore your Grace
may well say I have lost it.
DON PEDRO: You have put him down, lady; you have put him
250   down.
BEATRICE: So I would not he should do me, my lord, lest I should
prove the mother of fools. I have brought Count Claudio,
whom you sent me to seek.
DON PEDRO: Why, how now, count? Wherefore are you sad?
255 CLAUDIO: Not sad, my lord.
DON PEDRO: How then? sick?
CLAUDIO: Neither, my lord.
BEATRICE: The count is neither sad, nor sick, nor merry, nor well;
but civil count—civil as an orange,[33] and something of that
260   jealous complexion.
DON PEDRO: I' faith, lady, I think your blazon to be true; though
I'll be sworn, if he be so, his conceit is false. Here, Claudio, I
have wooed in thy name, and fair Hero is won. I have broke
with her father, and his good will obtained. Name the day of
265   marriage, and God give thee joy!

[28]*make her disappear*

[29]*other side of the world [see glossary]*

[30]*the legendary priest-king of Africa*

[31]*great ruler of Mongolia*

[32]*a half-woman, half-monster of Greek mythology*

[33]*close to yellow, the color associated with jealousy*

LEONATO: Count, take of me my daughter, and with her my fortunes. His Grace hath made the match, and all grace say Amen to it!

BEATRICE: Speak, count, 'tis your cue.

270 CLAUDIO: Silence is the perfectest herald of joy. I were but little happy if I could say how much. Lady, as you are mine, I am yours. I give away myself for you and dote upon the exchange.

BEATRICE: Speak, cousin; or, if you cannot, stop his mouth
275   with a kiss and let not him speak neither.

DON PEDRO: In faith, lady, you have a merry heart.

BEATRICE: Yea, my lord; I thank it, poor fool, it keeps on the windy side of care. My cousin tells him in his ear that he is in her heart.

280 CLAUDIO: And so she doth, cousin.

BEATRICE: Good Lord, for alliance! Thus goes every one to the world[34] but I, and I am sunburnt.[35] I may sit in a corner and cry 'Heigh-ho for a husband!'

DON PEDRO: Lady Beatrice, I will get you one.

285 BEATRICE: I would rather have one of your father's getting. Hath your Grace ne'er a brother like you? Your father got excellent husbands, if a maid could come by them.

DON PEDRO: Will you have me, lady?

BEATRICE: No, my lord, unless I might have another for work-
290   ing days: your Grace is too costly to wear every day. But I beseech your Grace pardon me. I was born to speak all mirth and no matter.

DON PEDRO: Your silence most offends me, and to be merry best becomes you, for out o' question you were born in
295   a merry hour.

BEATRICE: No, sure, my lord, my mother cried; but then there was a star danced, and under that was I born. Cousins, God give you joy!

LEONATO: Niece, will you look to those things I told you of?

300 BEATRICE: I cry you mercy, uncle, By your Grace's pardon.

Exit Beatrice.

DON PEDRO: By my troth, a pleasant-spirited lady.

LEONATO: There's little of the melancholy element in her, my lord. She is never sad but when she sleeps; and not ever sad then; for I have heard my daughter say she hath often
305   dreamt of unhappiness and waked herself with laughing.

DON PEDRO: She cannot endure to hear tell of a husband.

[34] *i.e., everyone is getting married*

[35] *no longer fair*

LEONATO: O, by no means! She mocks all her wooers out of suit.

DON PEDRO: She were an excellent wife for Benedick.

LEONATO: O Lord, my lord! if they were but a week married, they
310   would talk themselves mad.

DON PEDRO: County Claudio, when mean you to go to church?

CLAUDIO: To-morrow, my lord. Time goes on crutches till love
have all his rites.

LEONATO: Not till Monday, my dear son, which is hence just sev-
315   ennight; and a time too brief too, to have all things answer
my mind.

DON PEDRO: Come, you shake the head at so long a breathing;
but I warrant thee, Claudio, the time shall not go dully by
us. I will in the interim undertake one of Hercules' labours,
320   which is, to bring Signior Benedick and the Lady Beatrice
into a mountain of affection the one with the other. I would
fain[36] have it a match, and I doubt not but to fashion it if
you three will but minister such assistance as I shall give
you direction.

[36]*gladly*

325 LEONATO: My lord, I am for you, though it cost me ten nights'
watchings.

CLAUDIO: And I, my lord.

DON PEDRO: And you too, gentle Hero?

HERO: I will do any modest office, my lord, to help my cousin to
330   a good husband.

DON PEDRO: And Benedick is not the unhopefullest husband that
I know. Thus far can I praise him: he is of a noble strain, of
approved valour, and confirmed honesty. I will teach you
how to humour your cousin, that she shall fall in love with
335   Benedick; and I, *[To Leonato and Claudio]* with your two
helps, will so practice on Benedick that, in despite of his
quick wit and his queasy stomach, he shall fall in love with
Beatrice. If we can do this Cupid is no longer an archer; his
glory shall be ours, for we are the only love-gods. Go in with
340   me, and I will tell you my drift.   *Exeunt.*

SCENE II
[A Hall in Leonato's House]

Enter [Don] John and Borachio.

DON JOHN: It is so. The Count Claudio shall marry the daughter of Leonato.

BORACHIO: Yea, my lord; but I can cross it.

DON JOHN: Any bar, any cross, any impediment will be medici-
5   nable to me. I am sick in displeasure to him, and what-
soever comes athwart[37] his affection ranges evenly with
mine. How canst thou cross this marriage?

BORACHIO: Not honestly, my lord, but so covertly that no dis-
honesty shall appear in me.

10 DON JOHN: Show me briefly how.

BORACHIO: I think I told your lordship, a year since, how much
I am in the favour of Margaret, the waiting gentlewoman
to Hero.

DON JOHN: I remember.

15 BORACHIO: I can, at any unseasonable instant of the night,
appoint her to look out at her lady's chamber window.

DON JOHN: What life is in that to be the death of this marriage?

BORACHIO: The poison of that lies in you to temper. Go you to
20   the prince your brother; spare not to tell him that he hath
wronged his honour in marrying the renowned Claudio
whose estimation do you mightily hold up, to a contami-
nated stale,[38] such a one as Hero.

DON JOHN: What proof shall I make of that?

25 BORACHIO: Proof enough to misuse the prince, to vex Claudio,
to undo Hero, and kill Leonato. Look you for any other
issue?

DON JOHN: Only to despite them I will endeavour anything.

BORACHIO: Go then; find a meet hour to draw Don Pedro and
30   the Count Claudio alone; tell them that you know that
Hero loves me; intend a kind of zeal both to the prince
and Claudio, as—in love of your brother's honour, who
hath made this match, and his friend's reputation, who is
thus like to be cozened[39] with the semblance of a maid—
35   that you have discovered thus. They will scarcely believe
this without trial. Offer them instances; which shall bear
no less likelihood than to see me at her chamber win-

[37]*against*

[38]*prostitute*

[39]*cheated, deceived*

dow, hear me call Margaret, Hero, hear Margaret term me
Claudio[40]; and bring them to see this the very night before
40   the intended wedding—for in the meantime I will so fashion
the matter that Hero shall be absent—and there shall appear
such seeming truth of Hero's disloyalty that jealousy shall be
called assurance and all the preparation overthrown.

DON JOHN: Grow this to what adverse issue it can, I will put it
45   in practice. Be cunning in the working this, and thy fee is a
thousand ducats.

BORACHIO: Be you constant in the accusation, and my cunning
shall not shame me.

DON JOHN: I will presently go learn their day of marriage.

[Exeunt.]

SCENE III
[Leonato's Garden]

Enter Benedick alone.

BENEDICK: *[Enter Boy.]* Boy!

BOY: Signior?

BENEDICK: In my chamber window lies a book. Bring it hither to
me in the orchard.

5   BOY: I am here already, my lord.

BENEDICK: I know that, but I would have thee hence and here
again. *[Exit Boy.]* I do much wonder that one man, see-
ing how much another man is a fool when he dedicates
his behaviours to love, will, after he hath laughed at such
10   shallow follies in others, become the argument of his own
scorn by falling in love; and such a man is Claudio. I have
known when there was no music with him but the drum
and the fife;[41] and now had he rather hear the tabor and the
pipe.[42] I have known when he would have walked ten mile
15   afoot to see a good armour; and now will he lie ten nights
awake carving the fashion of a new doublet.[43] He was wont
to speak plain and to the purpose, like an honest man and a
soldier; and now is he turned orthography;[44] his words are a
very fantastical banquet—just so many strange dishes. May
20   I be so converted and see with these eyes? I cannot tell; I
think not. I will not be sworn but love may transform me
to an oyster; but I'll take my oath on it, till he have made

[40] *[Some critics sug-
gest this should
read Borachio
since Claudio will
overhear the con-
versation.]*

[41] *[instruments used
in war]*

[42] *i.e., dancing
music*

[43] *jacket*

[44] *formal spelling*

an oyster of me he shall never make me such a fool. One
woman is fair, yet I am well; another is wise, yet I am
25   well; another virtuous, yet I am well; but till all graces be
in one woman, one woman shall not come in my grace.
Rich she shall be, that's certain; wise, or I'll none; virtuous, or I'll never cheapen her; fair, or I'll never look on
her; mild, or come not near me; noble, or not I for an
30   angel; of good discourse, an excellent musician, and her
hair shall be of what colour it please God. Ha, the prince
and Monsieur Love! I will hide me in the arbour.

                                                    [Hides.]

Enter Prince [Don Pedro], Leonato, Claudio.

DON PEDRO: Come, shall we hear this music?
CLAUDIO: Yea, my good lord. How still the evening is, as
35   hushed on purpose to grace harmony!
DON PEDRO: See you where Benedick hath hid himself?
CLAUDIO: O, very well, my lord. The music ended, We'll fit the
kid-fox[45] with a pennyworth.[46]

Enter Balthasar with Music.

DON PEDRO: Come, Balthasar, we'll hear that song again.
40   BALTHASAR: O, good my lord, tax not so bad a voice
To slander music any more than once.
DON PEDRO: It is the witness[47] still of excellency
To put a strange face on his own perfection.
I pray thee, sing, and let me woo no more.
45   BALTHASAR: Because you talk of wooing, I will sing;
Since many a wooer doth commence his suit
To her he thinks not worthy, yet he woos,
Yet he will swear he loves.
DON PEDRO: Nay, pray thee, come;
50   Or, if thou wilt hold no longer argument,
Do it in notes.
BALTHASAR: Note this before my notes;
There's not a note of mine that's worth noting.
DON PEDRO: Why, these are very crotchets that he speaks;
55   Note, notes, forsooth, and nothing.   [Air]
BENEDICK: Now, divine air! now is his soul ravished! Is it not
strange that sheeps' guts[48] should hale souls out of men's
bodies? Well, a horn for my money, when all's done.

[45] *crafty young man*

[46] *i.e., a penny's worth of his own medicine*

[47] *habit*

[48] *[The strings of instruments were commonly made of sheep's intestines.]*

BALTHASAR: *The Song.*

60   Sigh no more, ladies, sigh no more,
            Men were deceivers ever,
        One foot in sea and one on shore,
            To one thing constant never:

        Then sigh not so, but let them go,
65   And be you blithe and bonny,
        Converting all your sounds of woe
            Into Hey nonny, nonny.

        Sing no more ditties, sing no moe,
            Of dumps so dull and heavey;
70   The fraud of men was ever so,
            Since summer first was leavy:

        Then sigh not so,&c.

DON PEDRO: By my troth, a good song.

BALTHASAR: And an ill singer, my lord.

75 DON PEDRO: Ha, no, no, faith! Thou singest well enough for a shift.[49]

BENEDICK: *[Aside]* An[50] he had been a dog that should have howled thus, they would have hanged him; and I pray God his bad voice bode no mischief. I had as live[51] have heard the

80   night raven, come what plague[52] could have come after it.

DON PEDRO: Yea, marry. Dost thou hear, Balthasar? I pray thee get us some excellent music; for to-morrow night we would have it at the Lady Hero's chamber window.

BALTHASAR: The best I can, my lord. *Exit Balthasar*

85 DON PEDRO: Do so. Farewell. Come hither, Leonato. What was it you told me of to-day? that your niece Beatrice was in love with Signior Benedick?

CLAUDIO: O, ay! *[Aside to Don Pedro]* Stalk[53] on, stalk on; the fowl[54] sits.—I did never think that lady would have loved

90   any man.

LEONATO: No, nor I neither; but most wonderful[55] that she should so dote on Signior Benedick, whom she hath in all outward behaviours seemed ever to abhor.

BENEDICK: *[Aside]* Is't possible? Sits the wind in that corner?

95 LEONATO: By my troth, my lord, I cannot tell what to think of it, but that she loves him with an enraged affection. It is past the infinite of thought.

[49]*i.e., lack of a better singer*

[50]*if*

[51]*rather*

[52]*[The raven was thought to announce the plague.]*

[53]*hunt*

[54]*[Claudio compares Benedick to a hunted bird.]*

[55]*surprising, amazing*

DON PEDRO: May be she doth but counterfeit.

CLAUDIO: Faith, like enough.

100 LEONATO: O God, counterfeit? There was never counterfeit of passion came so near the life of passion as she discovers it.

DON PEDRO: Why, what effects of passion shows she?

CLAUDIO: *[Aside]* Bait the hook well! This fish will bite.

105 LEONATO: What effects, my lord? She will sit you—you heard my daughter tell you how.

CLAUDIO: She did indeed.

DON PEDRO: How, how, I pray you? You amaze me. I would have thought her spirit had been invincible against all

110 assaults of affection.

LEONATO: I would have sworn it had, my lord—especially against Benedick.

BENEDICK: *[Aside]* I should think this a gull[56] but that the white-bearded fellow speaks it. Knavery cannot, sure,

115 hide himself in such reverence.

CLAUDIO: *[Aside]* He hath ta'en th' infection. Hold it up.

DON PEDRO: Hath she made her affection known to Benedick?

LEONATO: No, and swears she never will. That's her torment.

CLAUDIO: 'Tis true indeed. So your daughter says. 'Shall I,' says

120 she, 'that have so oft encountered him with scorn, write to him that I love him?'"

LEONATO: This says she now when she is beginning to write to him; for she'll be up twenty times a night, and there will she sit in her smock till she have writ a sheet of paper.

125 My daughter tells us all.

CLAUDIO: Now you talk of a sheet of paper, I remember a pretty jest your daughter told us of.

LEONATO: O, when she had writ it, and was reading it over, she found Benedick and Beatrice between the sheet?[57]

130 CLAUDIO: That.

LEONATO: O, she tore the letter into a thousand halfpence, railed at herself that she should be so immodest to write to one that she knew would flout her. 'I measure him,' says she, 'by my own spirit; for I should flout him if he

135 writ to me. Yea, though I love him, I should.'

CLAUDIO: Then down upon her knees she falls, weeps, sobs, beats her heart, tears her hair, prays, curses—O sweet Benedick! God give me patience!'

LEONATO: She doth indeed; my daughter says so. And the

[56]*trick*

[57]*"in the fold of the sheet of paper," but also "between the bedsheets"*

140   ecstasy hath so much overborne her that my daughter is sometime afeard she will do a desperate outrage to herself. It is very true.

DON PEDRO: It were good that Benedick knew of it by some other, if she will not discover it.

145 CLAUDIO: To what end? He would make but a sport of it and torment the poor lady worse.

DON PEDRO: An he should, it were an alms to hang him! She's an excellent sweet lady, and, out of all suspicion, she is virtuous.

150 CLAUDIO: And she is exceeding wise.

DON PEDRO: In everything but in loving Benedick.

LEONATO: O, my lord, wisdom and blood combating in so tender a body, we have ten proofs to one that blood hath the victory. I am sorry for her, as I have just cause, being her
155   uncle and her guardian.

DON PEDRO: I would she had bestowed this dotage on me. I would have daffed[58] all other respects and made her half myself. I pray you tell Benedick of it and hear what 'a will say.

160 LEONATO: Were it good, think you?

CLAUDIO: Hero thinks surely she will die; for she says she will die if he love her not, and she will die ere she make her love known, and she will die, if he woo her, rather than she will bate one breath of her accustomed crossness.

165 DON PEDRO: She doth well. If she should make tender[59] of her love, 'tis very possible he'll scorn it; for the man, as you know all hath a contemptible spirit.

CLAUDIO: He is a very proper man.

DON PEDRO: He hath indeed a good outward happiness.

170 CLAUDIO: Before God! and in my mind, very wise.

DON PEDRO: He doth indeed show some sparks that are like wit.

CLAUDIO: And I take him to be valiant.

DON PEDRO: As Hector,[60] I assure you; and in the managing of quarrels you may say he is wise, for either he avoids them
175   with great discretion, or undertakes them with a most Christianlike fear.

LEONATO: If he do fear God, 'a must necessarily keep peace. If he break the peace, he ought to enter into a quarrel with fear and trembling.

180 DON PEDRO: And so will he do; for the man doth fear God, howsoever it seems not in him by some large jests he will

[58]*thrown off*

[59]*offer*

[60]*a legendary Trojan warrior*

make. Well, I am sorry for your niece. Shall we go seek
Benedick and tell him of her love?

CLAUDIO: Never tell him, my lord. Let her wear it out with
185   good counsel.

LEONATO: Nay, that's impossible; she may wear her heart out
first.

DON PEDRO: Well, we will hear further of it by your daughter.
Let it cool the while. I love Benedick well, and I could
190   wish he would modestly examine himself to see how
much he is unworthy so good a lady.

LEONATO: My lord, will you walk? Dinner is ready.

CLAUDIO: If he do not dote on her upon this, I will never trust
my expectation.

DON PEDRO: Let there be the same net spread for her, and that
195   must your daughter and her gentlewomen carry. The
sport will be, when they hold one an opinion of another's
dotage, and no such matter. That's the scene that I would
see, which will be merely a dumb show.[61] Let us send her
to call him in to dinner.

> *Exeunt [Don Pedro, Claudio, and Leonato.]*

200 BENEDICK: This can be no trick. The conference[62] was sadly
borne;[63] they have the truth of this from Hero; they seem
to pity the lady. It seems her affections have their full
bent. Love me? Why, it must be requited. I hear how I
am censured.[64] They say I will bear myself proudly if I
205   perceive the love come from her. They say too that she
will rather die than give any sign of affection. I did never
think to marry. I must not seem proud. Happy are they
that hear their detractions and can put them to mending.
They say the lady is fair—'tis a truth, I can bear them
210   witness; and virtuous—'tis so, I cannot reprove it; and
wise, but for loving me—by my troth, it is no addition to
her wit, nor no great argument of her folly, for I will be
horribly in love with her. I may chance have some odd
quirks and remnants of wit broken on me because I have
215   railed so long against marriage. But doth not the appetite
alter? A man loves the meat in his youth that he cannot
endure in his age. Shall quips[65] and sentences[66] and these
paper bullets of the brain awe a man from the career[67] of
his humour?[68] No, the world must be peopled. When I
220   said I would die a bachelor, I did not think I should live
till I were married. Here comes Beatrice. By this day! she's
a fair lady: I do spy some marks of love in her.

[61]*pantomime that precedes a main play*

[62]*conversation*

[63]*carried out*

[64]*judged*

[65]*jokes*

[66]*wise sayings*

[67]*course*

[68]*will*

Enter Beatrice.

BEATRICE: Against my will I am sent to bid you come in to dinner.

225 BENEDICK: Fair Beatrice, I thank you for your pains.

BEATRICE: I took no more pains for those thanks than you take pains to thank me. If it had been painful, I would not have come.

BENEDICK: You take pleasure then in the message?

230 BEATRICE: Yea, just so much as you may take upon a knife's point, and choke a daw[69] withal. You have no stomach, signior? Fare you well.   *Exit.*

BENEDICK: Ha! 'Against my will I am sent to bid you come in to dinner.' There's a double meaning in that. 'I took no more
235   pains for those thanks than you took pains to thank me.' That's as much as to say, 'Any pains that I take for you is as easy as thanks.' If I do not take pity of her, I am a villain; if I do not love her, I am a Jew. I will go get her picture.

Exit.

[69] *a bird related to the crow*

ACT III

SCENE I
[Leonato's Orchard]

Enter Hero, and two gentlewomen, Margaret, and Ursula.

HERO: Good Margaret, run thee to the parlour.
    There shalt thou find my cousin Beatrice
    Proposing with the prince and Claudio.
    Whisper her ear and tell her, I and Ursula
5   Walk in the orchard, and our whole discourse
    Is all of her. Say that thou overheard'st us;
    And bid her steal into the pleached bower,
    Where honeysuckles, ripened by the sun,
    Forbid the sun to enter—like favourites,
10   Made proud by princes, that advance their pride
    Against that power that bred it. There will she hide her
    To listen our propose. This is thy office.
    Bear thee well in it and leave us alone.
MARGARET: I'll make her come, I warrant you, presently.
                                [Exit.]
15 HERO: Now, Ursula, when Beatrice doth come,
    As we do trace this alley up and down,
    Our talk must only be of Benedick.
    When I do name him, let it be thy part
    To praise him more than ever man did merit.
20   My talk to thee must be how Benedick
    Is sick in love with Beatrice. Of this matter
    Is little Cupid's crafty arrow made,
    That only wounds by hearsay. Now begin,

Enter Beatrice.
    For look where Beatrice like a lapwing[1] runs,
25   Close by the ground, to hear our conference.
                [Beatrice hides in the arbour.]

[1]*a bird that runs
along the ground*

41

URSULA: The pleasant'st angling is to see the fish
          Cut with her golden oars the silver stream.
          And greedily devour the treacherous bait.
          So angle we for Beatrice, who even now

²honeysuckle   30   Is couched in the woodbine² coverture.³

³cover   Fear you not my part of the dialogue.
HERO: Then go we near her, that her ear lose nothing
          Of the false sweet bait that we lay for it.
          No, truly, Ursula, she is too disdainful.

⁴hawks   35   I know her spirits are as coy and wild
          As haggards⁴ of the rock.
URSULA: But are you sure
          That Benedick loves Beatrice so entirely?
HERO: So says the prince, and my new-trothed lord.
40   URSULA: And did they bid you tell her of it, madam?
HERO: They did entreat me to acquaint her of it;
          But I persuaded them, if they loved Benedick,
          To wish him wrestle with affection,
          And never to let Beatrice know of it.
45   URSULA: Why did you so? Doth not the gentleman
          Deserve as full, as fortunate a bed
          As ever Beatrice shall couch upon?
HERO: O god of love! I know he doth deserve
          As much as may be yielded to a man:
50   But Nature never framed a woman's heart
          Of prouder stuff than that of Beatrice.
          Disdain and scorn ride sparkling in her eyes,
          Misprizing what they look on; and her wit
          Values itself so highly, that to her
55   All matter else seems weak. She cannot love,
          Nor take no shape nor project of affection,
          She is so self-endeared.
URSULA: Sure I think so;
          And therefore certainly it were not good
60   She knew his love, lest she'll make sport at it.
HERO: Why, you speak truth. I never yet saw man,
          How wise, how noble, young, how rarely featured,
          But she would spell him backward. If fair-faced,
          She would swear the gentleman should be her sister;
65   If black, why, Nature, drawing of an antique,
          Made a foul blot; if tall, a lance ill-headed;
          If low, an agate very vilely cut;

If speaking, why, a vane blown with all winds;
If silent, why, a block moved with none.
70   So turns she every man the wrong side out
And never gives to truth and virtue that
Which simpleness and merit purchaseth.
URSULA: Sure, sure, such carping is not commendable.
HERO: No, not to be so odd, and from all fashions,
75   As Beatrice is, cannot be commendable.
But who dare tell her so? If I should speak,
She would mock me into air; O, she would laugh me
Out of myself, press me to death with wit!
Therefore let Benedick, like covered fire,
80   Consume away in sighs, waste inwardly.
It were a better death than die with mocks,
Which is as bad as die with tickling.
URSULA: Yet tell her of it. Hear what she will say.
HERO: No; rather I will go to Benedick
85   And counsel him to fight against his passion.
And truly, I'll devise some honest slanders
To stain my cousin with. One doth not know
How much an ill word may empoison liking.
URSULA: O, do not do your cousin such a wrong!
90   She cannot be so much without true judgment,
Having so swift and excellent a wit
As she is prized to have, as to refuse
So rare a gentleman as Signior Benedick.
HERO: He is the only man of Italy,
95   Always excepted my dear Claudio.
URSULA: I pray you be not angry with me, madam,
Speaking my fancy: Signior Benedick,
For shape, for bearing, argument, and valour,
Goes foremost in report through Italy.
100 HERO: Indeed he hath an excellent good name.
URSULA: His excellence did earn it ere he had it.
When are you married, madam?
HERO: Why, every day to-morrow! Come, go in.
I'll show thee some attires, and have thy counsel
105   Which is the best to furnish me tomorrow.
URSULA: She's limed,⁵ I warrant you! We have caught her, madam.   ⁵*trapped*
HERO: If it prove so, then loving goes by haps;⁶
Some Cupid kills with arrows, some with traps.   ⁶*chance*

[Exeunt Hero and Ursula.]

BEATRICE: What fire is in mine ears? Can this be true?
110   Stand I condemned for pride and scorn so much?
     Contempt, farewell! and maiden pride, adieu!
        No glory lives behind the back of such.
     And, Benedick, love on; I will requite thee,
        Taming my wild heart to thy loving hand.
115   If thou dost love, my kindness shall incite thee
        To bind our loves up in a holy band;
     For others say thou dost deserve, and I
     Believe it better than reportingly.[7]   *Exit.*

[7] *i.e., as if it were only gossip*

SCENE II
[A Room in Leonato's House]

Enter Prince [Don Pedro], Claudio, Benedick, and Leonato.

DON PEDRO: I do but stay till your marriage be consummate,[8] and then go I toward Aragon.

CLAUDIO: I'll bring you thither, my lord, if you'll vouchsafe me.

5   DON PEDRO: Nay, that would be as great a soil in the new gloss of your marriage as to show a child his new coat and forbid him to wear it. I will only be bold with Benedick for his company; for, from the crown of his head to the sole of his foot, he is all mirth. He hath twice or thrice
10   cut Cupid's bowstring, and the little hangman dare not shoot at him. He hath a heart as sound as a bell; and his tongue is the clapper, for what his heart thinks, his tongue speaks.

BENEDICK: Gallants, I am not as I have been.

15   LEONATO: So say I. Methinks you are sadder.

CLAUDIO: I hope he be in love.

DON PEDRO: Hang him, truant! There's no true drop of blood in him to be truly touched with love. If he be sad, he wants money.

20   BENEDICK: I have the toothache.

DON PEDRO: Draw it.

BENEDICK: Hang it!

CLAUDIO: You must hang it first and draw it afterwards.

DON PEDRO: What? sigh for the toothache?

[8] *complete*

25 LEONATO: Where is but a humour or a worm.[9]

BENEDICK: Well, every one can master a grief, but he that has it.

CLAUDIO: Yet say I, he is in love.

DON PEDRO: There is no appearance of fancy in him, unless
it be a fancy that he hath to strange disguises; as to be a
30   Dutchman to-day, a Frenchman to-morrow; or in the shape
of two countries at once, as a German from the waist down-
ward, all slops,[10] and a Spaniard from the hip upward, no
doublet. Unless he have a fancy to this foolery, as it appears
he hath, he is no fool for fancy, as you would have it appear
35   he is.

CLAUDIO: If he be not in love with some woman, there is no
believing old signs. A' brushes his hat o' mornings. What
should that bode?

DON PEDRO: Hath any man seen him at the barber's?

40 CLAUDIO: No, but the barber's man hath been seen with him, and
the old ornament[11] of his cheek hath already stuffed tennis
balls.

LEONATO: Indeed he looks younger than he did, by the loss of a
beard.

45 DON PEDRO: Nay, a' rubs himself with civet.[12] Can you smell him
out by that?

CLAUDIO: That's as much as to say, the sweet youth's in love.

DON PEDRO: The greatest note of it is his melancholy.

CLAUDIO: And when was he wont to wash his face?

50 DON PEDRO: Yea, or to paint himself?[13] for the which I hear what
they say of him.

DON PEDRO: Indeed that tells a heavy tale for him. Conclude,
conclude, he is in love.

CLAUDIO: Nay, but I know who loves him.

55 DON PEDRO: That would I know too. I warrant, one that knows
him not.

CLAUDIO: Yes, and his ill conditions; and in despite of all, dies
for him.

DON PEDRO: She shall be buried with her face upwards.

60 BENEDICK: Yet is this no charm for the toothache. Old signior,
walk aside with me. I have studied eight or nine wise words
to speak to you, which these hobby-horses[14] must not hear.

[*Exeunt Benedick and Leonato.*]

DON PEDRO: For my life, to break with him about Beatrice!

CLAUDIO: 'Tis even so. Hero and Margaret have by this played
65   their parts with Beatrice, and then the two bears will not bite
one another when they meet.

---

[9]*two supposed causes of tooth-ache [see glossary]*

[10]*baggy pants*

[11]*his beard clippings*

[12]*musk-like perfume*

[13]*use makeup*

[14]*clowns*

Enter [Don] John the Bastard.

DON JOHN: My lord and brother, God save you.

DON PEDRO: Good den,[15] brother.

DON JOHN: If your leisure served, I would speak with you.

70   DON PEDRO: In private?

DON JOHN: If it please you. Yet Count Claudio may hear, for what I would speak of concerns him.

DON PEDRO: What's the matter?

DON JOHN: *[To Claudio]* Means your lordship to be married

75   tomorrow?

DON PEDRO: You know he does.

DON JOHN: I know not that, when he knows what I know.

CLAUDIO: If there be any impediment, I pray you discover it.

DON JOHN: You may think I love you not. Let that appear here-

80   after, and aim better at me by that I now will manifest. For my brother, I think he holds you well and in dear-ness of heart hath holp to effect your ensuing marriage—surely suit ill spent and labour ill bestowed!

DON PEDRO: Why, what's the matter?

85   DON JOHN: I came hither to tell you; and, circumstances short-ened, for she has been too long atalking of, the lady is disloyal.

CLAUDIO: Who? Hero?

DON JOHN: Even she—Leonato's Hero, your Hero, every man's

90   Hero.

CLAUDIO: Disloyal?

DON JOHN: The word is too good to paint out her wickedness. I could say she were worse; think you of a worse title, and I will fit her to it. Wonder not till further warrant. Go

95   but with me to-night, you shall see her chamber window ent'red, even the night before her wedding day. If you love her then, to-morrow wed her. But it would better fit your honour to change your mind.

CLAUDIO: May this be so?

100 DON PEDRO: I will not think it.

DON JOHN: If you dare not trust that you see, confess not that you know. If you will follow me, I will show you enough; and when you have seen more and heard more, proceed accordingly.

105 CLAUDIO: If I see anything to-night why I should not marry her

[15]*evening*

tomorrow, in the congregation where I should wed, there will I shame her.

DON PEDRO: And, as I wooed for thee to obtain her, I will join
110   with thee to disgrace her.

DON JOHN: I will disparage her no farther till you are my witnesses. Bear it coldly[16] but till midnight, and let the issue show itself.

DON PEDRO: O day untowardly turned!

115 CLAUDIO: O mischief strangely thwarting!

DON JOHN: O plague right well prevented! So will you say when you have seen the sequel.   *[Exeunt.]*

SCENE III
[A Street]

Enter Dogberry and his copartner [Verges] with the Watch.

DOGBERRY: Are you good men and true?

VERGES: Yea, or else it were pity but they should suffer salvation,[17] body and soul.

DOGBERRY: Nay, that were a punishment too good for them, if
5   they should have any allegiance in them, being chosen for the prince's watch.

VERGES: Well, give them their charge, neighbour Dogberry.

DOGBERRY: First, who think you the most desartless[18] man to be constable?

10 FIRST WATCHMAN: Hugh Oatcake, my lord, or George Seacoal; for they can write and read.

DOGBERRY: Come hither, neighbour Seacoal. God hath blessed you with a good name. To be a well-favoured man is the gift of fortune, but to write and read comes by nature.[19]

15 SECOND WATCHMAN: Both which, Master Constable—

DOGBERRY: You have. I knew it would be your answer. Well, for your favour, my lord, why, give God thanks and make no boast of it; and for your writing and reading, let that appear when there is no need of such vanity. You are thought here
20   to be the most senseless[20] and fit man for the constable of the watch. Therefore bear you the lanthorn. This is your charge: you shall comprehend[21] all vagrom[22] men; you are to bid any man stand, in the prince's name.

SECOND WATCHMAN: How if 'a will not stand?

[16]*quietly*

[17]*Dogberry's mistake for "damnation" [see glossary]*

[18]*mistake for "most deserving"*

[19]*[Dogberry means the opposite of what he says here.]*

[20]*sensible*

[21]*apprehend*

[22]*vagrant*

25 DOGBERRY: Why then, take no note of him, but let him go, and
        presently call the rest of the watch together and thank
        God you are rid of a knave.

    VERGES: If he will not stand when he is bidden, he is none of
        the prince's subjects.

30 DOGBERRY: True, and they are to meddle with none but the
        prince's subjects. You shall also make no noise in the
        streets; for for the watch to babble and to talk is most
        tolerable, and not to be endured.

    SECOND WATCHMAN: We will rather sleep than talk. We know
35   what belongs to a watch.

    DOGBERRY: Why, you speak like an ancient and most quiet
        watchman, for I cannot see how sleeping should offend.
        Only have a care that your bills[23] be not stolen. Well,
        you are to call at all the alehouses and bid those that are
40   drunk get them to bed.

    SECOND WATCHMAN: How if they will not?

    DOGBERRY: Why then, let them alone till they are sober. If they
        make you not then the better answer, you may say they
        are not the men you took them for.

45 SECOND WATCHMAN: Well, my lord.

    DOGBERRY: If you meet a thief, you may suspect him, by virtue
        of your office, to be no true man; and for such kind of
        men, the less you meddle or make with them, why, the
        more is for your honesty.

50 SECOND WATCHMAN: If we know him to be a thief, shall we not
        lay hands on him?

    DOGBERRY: Truly, by your office you may; but I think they that
        touch pitch[24] will be defiled. The most peaceable way for
        you, if you do take a thief, is to let him show himself what
55   he is, and steal[25] out of your company.

    VERGES: You have been always called a merciful man, partner.

    DOGBERRY: Truly, I would not hang a dog by my will, much
        more a man who hath any honesty in him.

    VERGES: If you hear a child cry in the night, you must call to
60   the nurse and bid her still it.

    SECOND WATCH: How if the nurse be asleep and will not hear
        us?

    DOGBERRY: Why then, depart in peace and let the child wake
        her with crying; for the ewe that will not hear her lamb
65   when it baes[26] will never answer a calf when he bleats.

    VERGES: 'Tis very true.

[23]weapons

[24]tar

[25]sneak

[26]baas

DOGBERRY: This is the end of the charge—you, constable, are to present[27] the prince's own person: if you meet the prince in the night, you may stay him.

70 VERGES: Nay, by'r lady, that I think 'a cannot.

DOGBERRY: Five shillings to one on't with any man that knows the statutes,[28] he may stay him! Marry, not without the prince be willing; for indeed the watch ought to offend no man, and it is an offence to stay a man against his will.

75 VERGES: By'r lady, I think it be so.

DOGBERRY: Ha, ah, ha! Well, masters, good night. An[29] there be any matter of weight[30] chances, call up me. Keep your fellows' counsels and your own, and good night. Come, neighbour.

80 SECOND WATCHMAN: Well, masters, we hear our charge. Let us go sit here upon the church bench till two, and then all to bed.

DOGBERRY: One word more, honest neighbours. I pray you watch about Signior Leonato's door; for the wedding being there tomorrow, there is a great coil[31] to-night. Adieu. Be vigi-

85 tant,[32] I beseech you.   *Exeunt [Dogberry, Verges]*

Enter Borachio and Conrade.

BORACHIO: What, Conrade!

SECOND WATCHMAN: *[Aside]* Peace! stir not!

BORACHIO: Conrade, I say!

CONRADE: Here, man. I am at thy elbow.

90 BORACHIO: Mass,[33] and my elbow itched! I thought there would a scab follow.

CONRADE: I will owe thee an answer for that; and now forward with thy tale.

BORACHIO: Stand thee close then under this penthouse,[34] for it drizzles rain, and I will, like a true drunkard, utter all to thee.

95

SECOND WATCHMAN: *[Aside]* Some treason, masters. Yet stand close.

BORACHIO: Therefore know I have earned of Don John a thousand

100 ducats.[35]

CONRADE: Is it possible that any villainy should be so dear?

BORACHIO: Thou shouldst rather ask if it were possible any villainy should not be so rich; for when rich villains have need of poor ones, poor ones may make what price they will.

105 CONRADE: I wonder at it.

[27]*represent [see glossary]*

[28]*laws*

[29]*if*

[30]*significant*

[31]*fuss*

[32]*vigilant*

[33]*"by the Mass" (an oath)*

[34]*canopy of leaves*

[35]*coins*

36ignorant

BORACHIO: That shows thou art unconfirmed.36 Thou knowest
that the fashion of a doublet, or a hat, or a cloak, is nothing to a man.

CONRADE: Yes, it is apparel.

110 BORACHIO: I mean the fashion.

CONRADE: es, the fashion is the fashion.

BORACHIO: Tush, I may as well say the fool's the fool. But seest
thou not what a deformed thief this fashion is?

FIRST WATCHMAN:, *[Aside]* I know that Deformed. He has been

115   a vile thief this seven year. He goes up and down like a
gentleman. I remember his name.

BORACHIO: Didst thou not hear somebody?

CONRADE: No, 'twas the vane on the house.

BORACHIO: Seest thou not, I say, what a deformed thief this

120   fashion is, how giddily he turns about all the hot bloods
between fourteen and five-and-thirty, sometimes fashion-
ing them like Pharaoh's soldiers in the reechy37 paint-
ing, sometimes like god Bel's38 priests in the old church
window, sometimes like the shaven Hercules in the

125   smirched39 worm-eaten tapestry, where his codpiece40
seems as massy as his club?

CONRADE: All this I see; and I see that the fashion wears out
more apparel than the man. But art not thou thyself giddy
with the fashion too, that thou hast shifted out of thy tale

130   into telling me of the fashion?

BORACHIO: Not so neither. But know that I have to-night
wooed Margaret, the Lady Hero's gentlewoman, by the
name of Hero. She leans me out at her mistress' chamber
window, bids me a thousand times good night—I tell this

135   tale vilely; I should first tell thee how the prince, Claudio
and my master, planted and placed and possessed by my
master Don John, saw afar off in the orchard this amiable
encounter.

CONRADE: And thought they Margaret was Hero?

BORACHIO: Two of them did, the prince and Claudio; but the

140   devil my master knew she was Margaret; and partly by
his oaths, which first possessed them, partly by the dark
night, which did deceive them, but chiefly by my villainy,
which did confirm any slander that Don John had made,

145   away went Claudio enraged; swore he would meet her, as
he was appointed, next morning at the temple, and there,
before the whole congregation, shame her with what he

37grimy

38the god Baal
(see glossary)

39soiled

40a protective case
on the front of a
man's pants

saw o'ernight and send her home again without a husband.

FIRST WATCHMAN: We charge you in the prince's name stand!

150 SECOND WATCHMAN: Call up the right master constable. We have
here recovered the most dangerous piece of lechery that ever
was known in the commonwealth.

FIRST WATCHMAN: And one Deformed is one of them. I know him;
a' wears a lock.[41]

155 CONRADE: Masters, masters—

SECOND WATCHMAN: You'll be made bring Deformed forth, I warrant you.

CONRADE: Masters—

SECOND WATCHMAN: Never speak; we charge you, let us obey you
160 to go with us.

BORACHIO: We are like to prove a goodly commodity, being taken
up of these men's bills.

CONRADE: A commodity in question, I warrant you. Come, we'll
obey you.   *Exeunt.*

[41] *long strand of hair*

SCENE IV
[A Room in Leonato's House]

Enter Hero, Margaret, and Ursula.

HERO: Good Ursula, wake my cousin Beatrice and desire her to
rise.

URSULA: I will, lady.

HERO: And bid her come hither.

5 URSULA: Well.   *[Exit.]*

MARGARET: Troth,[42] I think your other rebato[43] were better.

HERO: No, pray thee, good Meg, I'll wear this.

MARGARET: By my troth, is not so good; and I warrant your cousin
will say so.

10 HERO: My cousin 's a fool, and thou art another. I'll wear none
but this.

MARGARET: I like the new tire[44] within excellently, if the hair were
a thought browner; and your gown's a most rare fashion, i'
faith. I saw the Duchess of Milan's gown that they praise so.

15 HERO: O, that exceeds,[45] they say.

MARGARET: By my troth's but a nightgown in respect of yours—
cloth-o'-gold and cuts, and laced with silver, set with pearls
down sleeves, side-sleeves, and skirts, round underborne

[42] *in truth*

[43] *collar*

[44] *headdress*

[45] *is wonderful*

with a blush tinsel. But for a fine, quaint, graceful, and
20   excellent fashion, yours is worth ten on't.

HERO: God give me joy to wear it! for my heart is exceeding
heavy.

MARGARET: 'Twill be heavier soon by the weight of a man.

HERO: Fie upon thee! art not ashamed?

25 MARGARET: Of what, lady? of speaking honourably? Is not
marriage honourable in a beggar? Is not your lord honourable without marriage? I think you would have me
say, 'saving your reverence, a husband.' An bad thinking
do not wrest[46] true speaking, I'll offend nobody. Is there
30   any harm in 'the heavier for a husband'? None, I think,
an it be the right husband and the right wife. Otherwise
'tis light,[47] and not heavy. Ask my Lady Beatrice else. Here
she comes.

Enter Beatrice.

HERO: Good morrow, coz.

35 BEATRICE: Good morrow, sweet Hero.

HERO: Why, how now? Do you speak in the sick tune?

BEATRICE: I am out of all other tune, methinks.

MARGARET: Clap's into 'Light o' love.' That goes without a burden.[48] Do you sing it, and I'll dance it.

40 BEATRICE: Ye, 'Light o' love' with your heels! then, if your
husband have stables enough, you'll see he shall lack no
barns.[49]

MARGARET: O illegitimate construction! I scorn that with my
heels.

45 BEATRICE: 'Tis almost five o'clock, cousin; 'tis time you were
ready. By my troth, I am exceeding ill. Heigh-ho!

MARGARET: For a hawk, a horse, or a husband?

BEATRICE: For the letter that begins them all, H.

MARGARET: Well, an you be not turned Turk,[50] there's no more
50   sailing by the star.

BEATRICE: What means the fool, trow?[51]

MARGARET: Nothing I; but God send every one their heart's
desire!

HERO: These gloves the count sent me, they are an excellent
55   perfume.

BEATRICE: I am stuffed,[52] cousin; I cannot smell.

MARGARET: A maid, and stuffed! There's goodly catching of

---

[46]*distort, misinterpret*

[47]*immoral*

[48]*refrain*

[49]*i.e., if you have lots of room, you will have lots of children*

[50]*i.e., if you have gone back on your old vows (see glossary)*

[51]*do you think*

[52]*Beatrice means "congested," but Margaret plays on a meaning of "pregnant."*

cold.

BEATRICE: O, God help me! God help me! How long have you
60   professed apprehension?[53]

MARGARET: Ever since you left it. Doth not my wit become me
rarely?

BEATRICE: It is not seen enough. You should wear it in your cap.
By my troth, I am sick.

65   MARGARET: Get you some of this distilled Carduus Benedictus[54]
and lay it on your heart. It is the only thing for a qualm.[55]

HERO: There thou prickest her with a thistle.

BEATRICE: Benedictus? Why Benedictus? You have some moral in
this Benedictus?

70   MARGARET: Moral? No, by my troth, I have no moral meaning;
I meant, plain holy thistle. You may think perchance that I
think you are in love. Nay, by'r lady, I am not such a fool
to think what I list;[56] nor I list not to think what I can; nor
indeed I cannot think, if I would think my heart out of
75   thinking, that you are in love, or that you will be in love, or
that you can be in love. Yet Benedick was such another, and
now is he become a man. He swore he would never marry;
and yet now, in despite of his heart, he eats his meat without
grudging; and how you may be converted I know not, but
80   methinks you look with your eyes as other women do.

BEATRICE: What pace is this that thy tongue keeps?

MARGARET: Not a false gallop.[57]

Enter Ursula

URSULA: Madam, withdraw. The prince, the count, Signior
Benedick, Don John, and all the gallants of the town are
85   come to fetch you to church.

HERO: Help to dress me, good coz, good Meg, good Ursula.

Exeunt.

[53]*practiced witti-
ness*

[54]*an herb also
called "holy
thistle"*

[55]*sickness*

[56]*please*

[57]*a term meaning
"fast trot"; in this
case, "false" also
means "mistaken"*

SCENE V
[Another Room in Leonato's House]

Enter Leonato, Constable [Dogberry] and Headborough [Verges.]

LEONATO: What would you with me, honest neighbour?

DOGBERRY: Marry, my lord, I would have some confidence[58] with you that decerns[59] you nearly.

LEONATO: Brief, I pray you; for you see it is a busy time with
5   me.

DOGBERRY: Marry, this it is, my lord.

VERGES: Yes, in truth it is, my lord.

LEONATO: What is it, my good friends?

DOGBERRY: Goodman Verges, my lord, speaks a little off the
10   matter—an old man, my lord, and his wits are not so
blunt[60] as, God help, I would desire they were; but, in
faith, honest as the skin between his brows.

VERGES: Yes, I thank God I am as honest as any man living that
is an old man and no honester than I.

15 DOGBERRY: Comparisons are odorous.[61] Palabras,[62] neighbour
Verges.

LEONATO: Neighbours, you are tedious.

DOGBERRY: It pleases your worship to say so, but we are the
poor Duke's officers; but truly, for mine own part, if I
20   were as tedious[63] as a king, I could find in my heart to
bestow it all of your worship.

LEONATO: All thy tediousness on me, ah?

DOGBERRY: Yea, in 'twere a thousand pound more than 'tis; for
I hear as good exclamation[64] on your worship as of any
25   man in the city; and though I be but a poor man, I am
glad to hear it.

VERGES: And so am I.

LEONATO: I would fain know what you have to say.

VERGES: Marry, my lord, our watch to-night, excepting your
30   worship's presence, ha' ta'en a couple of as arrant knaves
as any in Messina.

DOGBERRY: A good old man, my lord; he will be talking. As
they say, 'When the age is in, the wit is out.' God help us!
it is a world to see! Well said, i' faith, neighbour Verges.
35   Well, God's a good man. An two men ride of a horse,
one must ride behind. An honest soul, i' faith, my lord,
by my troth he is, as ever broke bread; but God is to be

[58]*conference
(see glossary)*

[59]*concerns*

[60]*sharp*

[61]*odious*

[62]*from pocos pala-
bris, Spanish for
"few words"*

[63]*Dogberry mis-
takes "tedious" for
a word meaning
"wealthy."*

[64]*acclamation*

worshipped; all men are not alike, alas, good neighbour!

LEONATO: Indeed, neighbour, he comes too short of you.

40 DOGBERRY: Gifts that God gives.

LEONATO: I must leave you.

DOGBERRY: One word, my lord. Our watch, my lord, have indeed comprehended two aspicious[65] persons, and we would have them this morning examined before your worship.

65*auspicious*

45 LEONATO: Take their examination yourself and bring it me. I am now in great haste, as it may appear unto you.

DOGBERRY: It shall be suffigance.[66]

66*sufficient*

LEONATO: Drink some wine ere you go. Fare you well.

[Enter a Messenger.]

MESSENGER: My lord, they stay for you to give your daughter to

50   her husband.

LEONATO: I'll wait upon them. I am ready.

[Exeunt Leonato and Messenger.]

DOGBERRY: Go, good partner, go get you to Francis Seacoal; bid him bring his pen and inkhorn to the jail. We are now to examination these men.

55 VERGES: And we must do it wisely.

DOGBERRY: We will spare for no wit, I warrant you. Here's that shall drive some of them to a non-come.[67] Only get the learned writer to set down our excommunication,[68] and meet me at the jail.

67*mistake for "non-plus," meaning "state of confusion"*

Exeunt.

68*communication*

ACT IV

SCENE I
[A Church]

Enter Prince [Don Pedro], Bastard [Don John], Leonato, Friar [Francis], Claudio, Benedick, Hero, Beatrice, [and Attendants.]

LEONATO: Come, Friar Francis, be brief. Only to the plain form of marriage, and you shall recount their particular duties afterwards.

FRIAR: You come hither, my lord, to marry this lady?

5 CLAUDIO: No.

LEONATO: To be married to her. Friar, you come to marry her.

FRIAR: Lady, you come hither to be married to this count?

HERO: I do.

FRIAR: If either of you know any inward impediment why you
10   should not be conjoined, I charge you on your souls to utter it.

CLAUDIO: Know you any, Hero?

HERO: None, my lord.

FRIAR: Know you any, count?

15 LEONATO: I dare make his answer—none.

CLAUDIO: O, what men dare do! what men may do! what men daily do, not knowing what they do!

BENEDICK: How now? interjections? Why then, some be of laughing, as, ah, ha, he![1]

20 CLAUDIO: Stand thee by, friar. Father, by your leave:
    Will you with free and unconstrained soul
    Give me this maid your daughter?

LEONATO: As freely, son, as God did give her me.

CLAUDIO: And what have I to give you back whose worth
25   May counterpoise[2] this rich and precious gift?

DON PEDRO: Nothing, unless you render her again.

CLAUDIO: Sweet prince, you learn me noble thankfulness.

[1] *[Benedick quotes a popular grammar book in response to Claudio's interjections.]*

[2] *match*

57

There, Leonato, take her back again.
Give not this rotten orange to your friend.
30   She's but the sign and semblance of her honour.
Behold how like a maid she blushes here!
O, what authority and show of truth
Can cunning sin cover itself withal!
Comes not that blood as modest evidence
35   To witness simple virtue. Would you not swear,
All you that see her, that she were a maid
By these exterior shows? But she is none:
She knows the heat of a luxurious bed;
Her blush is guiltiness, not modesty.
40 LEONATO: What do you mean, my lord?
CLAUDIO: Not to be married,
    Not to knit my soul to an approved³ wanton.⁴
LEONATO: Dear my lord, if you, in your own proof,
    Have vanquished the resistance of her youth
45   And made defeat of her virginity—
CLAUDIO: I know what you would say. If I have known her,
    You will say she did embrace me as a husband,
    And so extenuate⁵ the forehand⁶ sin. No, Leonato,
    I never tempted her with word too large,
50   But, as a brother to his sister, showed
    Bashful sincerity and comely love.
HERO: And seemed I ever otherwise to you?
CLAUDIO: Out on the seeming! I will write against it.
    You seem to me as Dian⁷ in her orb,⁸
55   As chaste as is the bud ere it be blown;⁹
    But you are more intemperate in your blood
    Than Venus,¹⁰ or those pamp'red animals
    That rage in savage sensuality.
HERO: Is my lord well that he doth speak so wide?¹¹
60 LEONATO: Sweet prince, why speak not you?
DON PEDRO: What should I speak?
    I stand dishonoured that have gone about
    To link my dear friend to a common stale.
LEONATO: Are these things spoken, or do I but dream?
65 DON JOHN: My lord, they are spoken, and these things are
    true.
BENEDICK: This looks not like a nuptial.
HERO: True! O God!
CLAUDIO: Leonato, stand I here?

³proved

⁴whore

⁵annul

⁶previously committed

⁷the Roman goddess of the moon and virginity

⁸the moon

⁹in full flower

¹⁰the goddess of sexual love

¹¹untruthfully

70   Is this the prince?
       Is this the prince's brother?
       Is this face Hero's?
       Are our eyes our own?
LEONATO: All this is so; but what of this, my lord?
75 CLAUDIO: Let me but move one question to your daughter,
       And by that fatherly and kindly power
       That you have in her, bid her answer truly.
LEONATO: I charge thee do so, as thou art my child.
HERO: O, God defend me! How am I beset!
80   What kind of catechising[12] call you this?
CLAUDIO: To make you answer truly to your name.
HERO: Is it not Hero? Who can blot that name
       With any just reproach?
CLAUDIO: Marry, that can Hero!
85   Hero itself can blot out Hero's virtue.
       What man was he talked with you yesternight,
       Out at your window betwixt twelve and one?
       Now, if you are a maid, answer to this.
HERO: I talked with no man at that hour, my lord.
90 DON PEDRO: Why, then are you no maiden. Leonato,
       I am sorry you must hear. Upon my honour,
       Myself, my brother, and this grieved count
       Did see her, hear her, at that hour last night
       Talk with a ruffian at her chamber window,
95   Who hath indeed, most like a liberal villain,
       Confessed the vile encounters they have had
       A thousand times in secret.
DON JOHN: Fie, fie! they are not to be named, my lord—
       Not to be spoke of;
100   There is not chastity, enough in language
       Without offence to utter them. Thus, pretty lady,
       I am sorry for thy much misgovernment.
CLAUDIO: O Hero! what a Hero hadst thou been
       If half thy outward graces had been placed
105   About thy thoughts and counsels of thy heart!
       But fare thee well, most foul, most fair! Farewell,
       Thou pure impiety and impious purity!
       For thee I'll lock up all the gates of love,
       And on my eyelids shall conjecture[13] hang,
110   To turn all beauty into thoughts of harm,
       And never shall it more be gracious.

[12]*questioning (see glossary)*

[13]*suspicion*

LEONATO: Hath no man's dagger here a point for me?

[Hero swoons.]

BEATRICE: Why, how now, cousin? Wherefore sink you down?

DON JOHN: Come let us go. These things, come thus to light,
115   Smother her spirits up.

[Exeunt Don Pedro, Don John, and Claudio.]

BENEDICK: How doth the lady?

BEATRICE: Dead, I think. Help, uncle!
Hero! why, Hero! Uncle! Signior Benedick! Friar!

LEONATO: O Fate, take not away thy heavy hand!
120   Death is the fairest cover for her shame
That may be wished for.

BEATRICE: How now, cousin Hero?

FRIAR: Have comfort, lady.

LEONATO: Dost thou look up?

125 FRIAR: Yea, wherefore should she not?

LEONATO: Wherefore? Why, doth not every earthly thing
Cry shame upon her? Could she here deny
The story that is printed in her blood?
Do not live, Hero; do not ope thine eyes;
130   For, did I think thou wouldst not quickly die,
Thought I thy spirits were stronger than thy shames,
Myself would on the rearward of reproaches
Strike at thy life. Grieved I, I had but one?
Chid I for that at frugal nature's frame?
135   O, one too much by thee! Why had I one?
Why ever wast thou lovely in my eyes?
Why had I not with charitable hand
Took up a beggar's issue at my gates,
Who smirched thus and mired with infamy,
140   I might have said, 'No part of it is mine;
This shame derives itself from unknown loins?
But mine, and mine I loved, and mine I praised,
And mine that I was proud on—mine so much
That I myself was to myself not mine,
145   Valuing of her—why, she, O, she is fallen
Into a pit of ink, that the wide sea
Hath drops too few to wash her clean again,
And salt too little which may season give
To her foul tainted flesh!

150 BENEDICK: My lord, my lord, be patient.
For my part, I am so attired in wonder,
I know not what to say.

BEATRICE: O, on my soul, my cousin is belied![14]

BENEDICK: Lady, were you her bedfellow last night?

155 BEATRICE: No, truly, not; although, until last night, I have this
    twelvemonth been her bedfellow.

LEONATO: Confirmed, confirmed! O, that is stronger made
    Which was before barred up with ribs of iron!
    Would the two princes lie? and Claudio lie,

160   Who loved her so that, speaking of her foulness,
    Washed it with tears? Hence from her! let her die.

FRIAR: Hear me a little;
    For I have only been silent so long,
    And given way unto this course of fortune,

165   By noting of the lady. I have marked
    A thousand blushing apparitions
    To start into her face, a thousand innocent shames
    In angel whiteness beat away those blushes,
    And in her eye there hath appeared a fire

170   To burn the errors that these princes hold
    Against her maiden truth. Call me a fool;
    Trust not my reading nor my observation,
    Which with experimental seal doth warrant
    The tenour of my book;[15] trust not my age,

175   My reverence, calling, nor divinity,
    If this sweet lady lie not guiltless here
    Under some biting error.

LEONATO: Friar, it cannot be.
    Thou seest that all the grace that she hath left

180   Is that she will not add to her damnation
    A sin of perjury: she not denies it.
    Why seek'st thou then to cover with excuse
    That which appears in proper nakedness?

FRIAR: Lady, what man is he you are accused of?

185 HERO: They know that do accuse me; I know none.
    If I know more of any man alive
    Than that which maiden modesty doth warrant,
    Let all my sins lack mercy! O my father,
    Prove you that any man with me conversed

190   At hours unmeet, or that I yesternight
    Maintained the change of words with any creature,
    Refuse me, hate me, torture me to death!

FRIAR: There is some strange misprision[16] in the princes.

BENEDICK: Two of them have the very bent of honour;

195   And if their wisdoms be misled in this,

[14]*betrayed*

[15]*i.e., which backs up what I have read with experience*

[16]*mistake*

The practice of it lives in Don John the bastard,
Whose spirits toil in frame of villainies.
LEONATO: I know not. If they speak but truth of her,
These hands shall tear her. If they wrong her honour,
200   The proudest of them shall well hear of it.
Time hath not yet so dried this blood of mine,
Nor age so eat up my invention,
Nor fortune made such havoc of my means,
Nor my bad life reft me so much of friends,
205   But they shall find awaked in such a kind
Both strength of limb and policy of mind,
Ability in means, and choice of friends,
To quit me of them thoroughly.
FRIAR: Pause awhile
210   And let my counsel sway you in this case.
Your daughter here the princes left for dead,
Let her awhile be secretly kept in,
And publish it that she is dead indeed;
Maintain a mourning ostentation,[17]
215   And on your family's old monument
Hang mournful epitaphs, and do all rites
That appertain unto a burial.
LEONATO: What shall become of this? What will this do?
FRIAR: Marry, this well carried shall on her behalf
220   Change slander to remorse. That is some good.
But not for that dream I on this strange course,
But on this travail[18] look for greater birth.
She dying, as it must be so maintained,
Upon the instant that she was accused,
225   Shall be lamented, pitied, and excused
Of every hearer; for it so falls out
That what we have we prize not to the worth
Whiles we enjoy it, but being lacked and lost,
Why, then we rack the value, then we find
230   The virtue that possession would not show us
Whiles it was ours. So will it fare with Claudio.
When he shall hear she died upon his words,
The idea of her life shall sweetly creep
Into his study of imagination,
235   And every lovely organ of her life
Shall come apparelled in more precious habit,
More moving, delicate, and full of life,

[17] *display*

[18] *both "work" and "childbirth"*

Into the eye and prospect of his soul
Than when she lived indeed. Then shall he mourn
240   If ever love had interest in his liver[19]
And wish he had not so accused her
No, though he thought his accusation true.
Let this be so, and doubt not but success
Will fashion the event in better shape
245   Than I can lay it down in likelihood.
But if all aim but this be levelled false,
The supposition of the lady's death
Will quench the wonder of her infamy.
And if it sort not well, you may conceal her,
250   As best befits her wounded reputation,
In some reclusive and religious life,
Out of all eyes, tongues, minds, and injuries.

BENEDICK: Signior Leonato, let the friar advise you;
And though you know my inwardness and love
255   Is very much unto the prince and Claudio,
Yet, by mine honour, I will deal in this
As secretly and justly as your soul
Should with your body.

LEONATO: Being that I flow in grief,
260   The smallest twine may lead me.

FRIAR: 'Tis well consented. Presently away;
For to strange sores strangely they strain the cure.
Come, lady, die to live. This wedding day
Perhaps is but prolonged.
265   Have patience and endure.

[Exeunt all but Benedick and Beatrice.]

BENEDICK: Lady Beatrice, have you wept all this while?

BEATRICE: Yea, and I will weep a while longer.

BENEDICK: I will not desire that.

BEATRICE: You have no reason. I do it freely.

270 BENEDICK: Surely I do believe your fair cousin is wronged.

BEATRICE: Ah, how much might the man deserve of me that would right her!

BENEDICK: Is there any way to show such friendship?

BEATRICE: A very even way, but no such friend.

275 BENEDICK: May a man do it?

BEATRICE: It is a man's office, but not yours.

BENEDICK: I do love nothing in the world so well as you. Is not that strange?

[19] *[supposed to be the organ in which passion originated]*

BEATRICE: As strange as the thing I know not. It were as pos-
280   sible for me to say I loved nothing so well as you. But
believe me not; and yet I lie not. I confess nothing, nor I
deny nothing. I am sorry for my cousin.

BENEDICK: By my sword, Beatrice, thou lovest me.

BEATRICE: Do not swear, and eat it.

285 BENEDICK: I will swear by it that you love me, and I will make
him eat it that says I love not you.

BEATRICE: Will you not eat your word?

BENEDICK: With no sauce that can be devised to it. I protest
I love thee.

290 BEATRICE: Why then, God forgive me!

BENEDICK: What offence, sweet Beatrice?

BEATRICE: You have stayed me in a happy hour. I was about to
protest I loved you.

BENEDICK: And do it with all thy heart.

295 BEATRICE: I love you with so much of my heart that none is
left to protest.

BENEDICK: Come, bid me do anything for thee.

BEATRICE: Kill Claudio.

BENEDICK: Ha! not for the wide world!

300 BEATRICE: You kill me to deny it. Farewell.

BENEDICK: Tarry, sweet Beatrice.

BEATRICE: I am gone, though I am here. There is no love in
you. Nay, I pray you let me go.

BENEDICK: Beatrice—

305 BEATRICE: In faith, I will go.

BENEDICK: We'll be friends first.

BEATRICE: You dare easier be friends with me than fight with
mine enemy.

BENEDICK: Is Claudio thine enemy?

310 BEATRICE: Is he not approved in the height a villain, that hath
slandered, scorned, dishonoured my kinswoman? O that
I were a man! What, bear her in hand until they come to
take hands, and then with public accusation, uncovered
slander, unmitigated rancour—O God, that I were a man!

315   I would eat his heart in the market place.

BENEDICK: Hear me, Beatrice!

BEATRICE: Talk with a man out at a window! — A proper saying!

BENEDICK: Nay, but Beatrice—

320 BEATRICE: Sweet Hero! She is wronged, she is sland'red, she
is undone.

BENEDICK: Beat—

BEATRICE: Princes and counties! Surely a princely testimony, a
goodly count, Count Comfect,²⁰ a sweet gallant surely! O

325   that I were a man for his sake! or that I had any friend would
be a man for my sake! But manhood is melted into courtesies, valour into compliment, and men are only turned into
tongue, and trim ones too. He is now as valiant as Hercules
that only tells a lie,and swears it. I cannot be a man with

330   wishing; therefore I will die a woman with grieving.

BENEDICK: Tarry, good Beatrice. By this hand, I love thee.

BEATRICE: Use it for my love some other way than swearing by it.

BENEDICK: Think you in your soul the Count Claudio hath
wronged Hero?

335 BEATRICE: Yea, as sure is I have a thought or a soul.

BENEDICK: Enough, I am engaged, I will challenge him. I will kiss
your hand, and so I leave you. By this hand, Claudio shall
render me a dear account. As you hear of me, so think of
me. Go comfort your cousin. I must say she is dead—and so

340   farewell.   *[Exeunt.]*

SCENE II
[A Prison]

*Enter the constables [Dogberry, Verges], Borachio [the Sexton, and
the Watch, with Conrade.]*

DOGBERRY: Is our whole dissembly²¹ appeared?

VERGES: O, a stool and a cushion for the sexton.

SEXTON: Which be the malefactors?²²

DOGBERRY: Marry, that am I and my partner.

5 VERGES: Nay, that's certain. We have the exhibition²³ to examine.

SEXTON: But which are the offenders that are to be examined? Let
them come before master constable.

DOGBERRY: Yea, marry, let them come before me. What is your
name, friend?

10 BORACHIO: Borachio.

DOGBERRY: Pray write down Borachio. Yours, sirrah?

CONRADE: I am a gentleman, sir, and my name is Conrade.

DOGBERRY: Write down master gentleman Conrade. Masters, do
you serve God?

15 BOTH: Yea, sir, we hope.

²⁰*"Count Candy"*

²¹*a mistake for
"assembly"
(see glossary)*

²²*"evildoers," but
Dogberry assumes
that "malefactor"
is a title for those
in authority*

²³*a mistake for
"evidence"*

DOGBERRY: Write down that they hope they serve God; and write God first, for God defend but God should go before such villains! Masters, it is proved already that you are little better than false knaves, and it will go near to be
20   thought so shortly. How answer you for yourselves?

CONRADE: Marry, sir, we say we are none.

DOGBERRY: A marvellous witty fellow, I assure you; but I will go about with him. Come you hither, sirrah.[24] A word in your ear. Sir, I say to you, it is thought you are false
25   knaves.

BORACHIO: Sir, I say to you we are none.

DOGBERRY: Well, stand aside. Fore God, they are both in a tale.[25] Have you writ down that they are none?

SEXTON: Master Constable, you go not the way to examine.
30   You must call forth the watch that are their accusers.

DOGBERRY: Yea, marry, that's the eftest[26] way. Let the watch come forth. Masters, I charge you in the prince's name accuse these men.

FIRST WATCHMAN: This man said, sir, that Don John the
35   prince's brother, was a villain.

DOGBERRY: Write down Prince Don John a villain. Why, this is flat perjury, to call a prince's brother villain.

BORACHIO: Master constable—

DOGBERRY: Pray thee, fellow, peace. I do not like thy look, I
40   promise thee.

SEXTON: What heard you him say else?

SECOND WATCHMAN: Marry, that he had received a thousand ducats of Don John for accusing the Lady Hero wrongfully.

45 DOGBERRY: Flat burglary as ever was committed.

VERGES: Yea, by the mass, that it is.

SEXTON: What else, fellow?

FIRST WATCHMAN: And that Count Claudio did mean, upon his words, to disgrace Hero before the whole assembly, and
50   not marry her.

DOGBERRY: O villain! thou wilt be condemned into everlasting redemption[27] for this.

SEXTON: What else?

WATCHMEN: This is all.

55 SEXTON: And this is more, masters, than you can deny. Prince Don John is this morning secretly stolen away. Hero was in this manner accused, in this manner refused, and upon

[24] a term for an inferior person

[25] in agreement

[26] most convenient

[27] a mistake for damnation

the grief of this suddenly died. Master constable, let these
men be bound and brought to Leonato's. I will go before and
60   show him their examination.   *[Exit.]*

DOGBERRY: Come, let them be opinioned.[28]

VERGES: Let them be in the hands—

CONRADE: Off, coxcomb!

DOGBERRY: God's my life, where's the sexton? Let him write down
65   the prince's officer coxcomb. Come, bind them—Thou
naughty varlet!

CONRADE: Away! you are an ass, you are an ass.

DOGBERRY: Dost thou not suspect[29] my place? Dost thou not suspect my years? O that he were here to write me down an ass!
70   But, masters, remember that I am an ass. Though it be not
written down, yet forget not that I am an ass. No, thou villain, thou art full of piety,[30] as shall be proved upon thee by
good witness. I am a wise fellow; and which is more, an officer; and which is more, a householder; and which is more,
75   as pretty a piece of flesh as any is in Messina, and one that
knows the law, go to! and a rich fellow enough, go to! and
a fellow that hath had losses; and one that hath two gowns
and everything handsome about him. Bring him away. O
that I had been writ down an ass!

                                                    Exeunt.

[28]*a mistake for
"pinioned"
(tied up)*

[29]*a mistake
for respect*

[30]*a mistake
for impiety*

ACT V

SCENE I
[Before Leonato's House]

Enter Leonato and his brother [Antonio].

ANTONIO: If you go on thus, you will kill yourself,
    And 'tis not wisdom thus to second grief
    Against yourself.
LEONATO: I pray thee cease thy counsel,
5   Which falls into mine ears as profitless
    As water in a sieve. Give not me counsel,
    Nor let no comforter delight mine ear
    But such a one whose wrongs do suit with mine.
    Bring me a father that so loved his child,
10   Whose joy of her is overwhelmed like mine,
    And bid him speak to me of patience.
    Measure his woe the length and breadth of mine,
    And let it answer every strain for strain,
    As thus for thus, and such a grief for such,
15   In every lineament, branch, shape, and form.
    If such a one will smile and stroke his beard,
    Bid sorrow wag,[1] cry 'hem' when he should groan,
    Patch grief with proverbs, make misfortune drunk
    With candle-wasters[2]—bring him yet to me,
20   And I of him will gather patience.
    But there is no such man; for, brother, men
    Can counsel and speak comfort to that grief
    Which they themselves not feel; but, tasting it,
    Their counsel turns to passion, which before
25   Would give preceptial[3] medicine to rage,
    Fetter[4] strong madness in a silken thread,
    Charm ache with air and agony with words.
    No, no! 'Tis all men's office to speak patience

[1] *act silly*

[2] *words that one stays up late reading*

[3] *of precepts, or wise advice*

[4] *bind*

To those that wring under the load of sorrow,
30   But no man's virtue nor sufficiency
To be so moral when he shall endure
The like himself. Therefore give me no counsel.
My griefs cry louder than advertisement.
ANTONIO: Therein do men from children nothing differ.
35 LEONATO: I pray thee peace. I will be flesh and blood;
For there was never yet philosopher
That could endure the toothache patiently,
However they have writ the style of gods
And made a push at chance and sufferance.
40 ANTONIO: Yet bend not all the harm upon yourself.
Make those that do offend you suffer too.
LEONATO: There thou speak'st reason. Nay, I will do so.
My soul doth tell me Hero is belied;
And that shall Claudio know; so shall the prince,
45   And all of them that thus dishonour her.

Enter Prince [Don Pedro] and Claudio.

ANTONIO: Here comes the prince and Claudio hastily.
DON PEDRO: Good den, good den.
CLAUDIO: Good day to both of you.
LEONATO: Hear you, my lords!
50 DON PEDRO: We have some haste, Leonato.
LEONATO: Some haste, my lord! well, fare you well, my lord.
Are you so hasty now? Well, all is one.
DON PEDRO: Nay, do not quarrel with us, good old man.
ANTONIO: If he could right himself with quarrelling,
55   Some of us would lie low.
CLAUDIO: Who wrongs him?
LEONATO: Marry, thou dost wrong me, thou dissembler, thou!
Nay, never lay thy hand upon thy sword;
I fear thee not.
60 CLAUDIO: Marry, beshrew my hand
If it should give your age such cause of fear.
In faith, my hand meant nothing to my sword.
LEONATO: Tush, tush, man! never fleer⁵ and jest at me.
I speak not like a dotard nor a fool,
65   As under privilege of age to brag
What I have done being young, or what would do,
Were I not old. Know, Claudio, to thy head,

⁵*mock*

Thou hast so wronged mine innocent child and me
That I am forced to lay my reverence by
70   And, with grey hairs and bruise of many days,
Do challenge thee to trial of a man.
I say thou hast belied mine innocent child;
Thy slander hath gone through and through her heart,
And she lied buried with her ancestors;
75   O, in a tomb where never scandal slept,
Save this of hers, framed by thy villainy!

CLAUDIO: My villainy?

LEONATO: Thine, Claudio; thine I say.

DON PEDRO: You say not right, old man.

80 LEONATO: My lord, my lord,
    I'll prove it on his body if he dare,
    Despite his nice fence[6] and his active practice,   *⁶swordplay*
    His May of youth and bloom of lustihood.

CLAUDIO: Away! I will not have to do with you.

LEONATO: Canst thou so daff me? Thou hast killed my child.
    If thou kill'st me, boy, thou shalt kill a man.

ANTONIO: He shall kill two of us, and men indeed.
    But that's no matter; let him kill one first.
85   Win me and wear me! Let him answer me.
    Come, follow me, boy.
    Come, sir boy, come follow me.
    Sir boy, I'll whip you from your foining[7] fence!   *⁷lunging*
    Nay, as I am a gentleman, I will.

90 LEONATO: Brother Anthony—

ANTONIO: Hold you content. What, man! I know them, yea,
    And what they weigh, even to the utmost scruple,
    Scambling, outfacing, fashion-monging boys,
    That lie and cog and flout, deprave and slander,
95   Go anticly,[8] and show outward hideousness,   *⁸bizarrely dressed*
    And speak off half a dozen dangerous words,
    How they might hurt their enemies, if they durst;
    And this is all.

LEONATO: But, brother Anthony—

100 ANTONIO: Come, 'tis no matter.
    Do not you meddle; let me deal in this.

DON PEDRO: Gentlemen both, we will not wake your patience.
    My heart is sorry for your daughter's death;
    But, on my honour, she was charged with nothing
105   But what was true, and very full of proof.

LEONATO: My lord, my lord—
DON PEDRO: I will not hear you.

Enter Benedick.

LEONATO: No? Come, brother, away!—I will be heard.
ANTONIO: And shall, or some of us will smart for it.
                              [Exeunt Leonato and Antonio]
110 DON PEDRO: See, see! Here comes the man we went to seek.
CLAUDIO: Now, signior, what news?
BENEDICK: Good day, my lord.
DON PEDRO: Welcome, signior. You are almost come to part
        almost a fray.
115 CLAUDIO: We had liked to have had our two noses snapped off
        with two old men without teeth.
DON PEDRO: Leonato and his brother. What think'st thou?
        Had we fought, I doubt we should have been too young
        for them.
120 BENEDICK: In a false quarrel there is no true valour. I came to
        seek you both.
CLAUDIO: We have been up and down to seek thee; for we are
        high-proof melancholy, and would fain have it beaten
        away. Wilt thou use thy wit?

⁹*sword-case*

125 BENEDICK: It is in my scabbard.⁹ Shall I draw it?
DON PEDRO: Dost thou wear thy wit by thy side?
CLAUDIO: Never any did so, though very many have been
        beside their wit. I will bid thee draw, as we do the min-
        strel—draw to pleasure us.
130 DON PEDRO: As I am an honest man, he looks pale. Art thou
        sick or angry?
CLAUDIO: What, courage, man! What though care killed a cat,
        thou hast mettle enough in thee to kill care.

¹⁰*mid-course*

BENEDICK: Sir, I shall meet your wit in the career¹⁰ an you
135   charge it against me. I pray you choose another subject.
CLAUDIO: Nay then, give him another staff; this last was broke
        cross.
DON PEDRO: By this light, he changes more and more. I think
        he be angry indeed.
140 CLAUDIO: If he be, he knows how to turn his girdle.
BENEDICK: Shall I speak a word in your ear?
CLAUDIO: God bless me from a challenge!

BENEDICK: *[Aside to Claudio]* You are a villain. I jest not; I will
make it good how you dare, with what you dare, and when
145   you dare. Do me right, or I will protest your cowardice. You
have killed a sweet lady, and her death shall fall heavy on
you. Let me hear from you.

CLAUDIO: Well, I will meet you, so I may have good cheer.

DON PEDRO: What, a feast, a feast?

150   CLAUDIO: I' faith, I thank him, he hath bid me to a calf's head[11]
and a capon,[12] the which if I do not carve most curiously, say
my knife's naught. Shall I not find a woodcock[13] too?

BENEDICK: Sir, your wit ambles well; it goes easily.

DON PEDRO: I'll tell thee how Beatrice praised thy wit the other
155   day. I said thou hadst a fine wit: 'True,' said she, 'a fine
little one.' 'No,' said I, 'a great wit.' 'Right,' says she, 'a great
gross one.' 'Nay,' said I, 'a good wit.' 'Just,' said she, 'it hurts
nobody.' 'Nay,' said I, 'the gentleman is wise.' 'Certain,' said
she, a wise gentleman.' 'Nay,' said I, 'he hath the tongues.'[14]
160   'That I believe' said she, 'for he swore a thing to me on
Monday night which he forswore on Tuesday morning.
There's a double tongue; there's two tongues.' Thus did she
an hour together transshape[15] thy particular virtues. Yet at
last she concluded with a sigh, thou wast the properest man
165   in Italy.

CLAUDIO: For the which she wept heartily and said she cared
not.

DON PEDRO: Yea, that she did; but yet, for all that, an if she did
not hate him deadly, she would love him dearly. The old
170   man's daughter told us all.

CLAUDIO: All, all! and moreover, God saw him when he was hid
in the garden.[16]

DON PEDRO: But when shall we set the savage bull's horns[17] on the
sensible Benedick's head?

175   CLAUDIO: Yea, and text underneath, 'Here dwells Benedick, the
married man'?

BENEDICK: Fare you well, boy; you know my mind. I will leave
you now to your gossiplike humour. You break jests as brag-
gards do their blades, which God be thanked hurt not. My
180   lord, for your many courtesies I thank you. I must discon-
tinue your company. Your brother the bastard is fled from
Messina. You have among you killed a sweet and innocent
lady. For my Lord Lackbeard there, he and I shall meet; and
till then peace be with him.   *[Exit.]*

---

[11]*a term for a fool (see glossary)*

[12]*eunuch*

[13]*a bird thought to be stupid*

[14]*knowledge of languages*

[15]*distort*

[16]*a reference to the Book of Genesis but also to Benedick hiding in the garden*

[17]*horns of a cuckold (see glossary)*

185 Don Pedro: He is in earnest.

Claudio: In most profound earnest; and, I'll warrant you, for the love of Beatrice.

Don Pedro: And hath challenged thee.

Claudio: Most sincerely.

190 Don Pedro: What a pretty thing man is when he goes in his doublet and hose and leaves off his wit!

Claudio: He is then a giant to an ape; but then is an ape a doctor to such a man.

Don Pedro: But, soft you, let me be! Pluck up, my heart, and be sad! Did he not say my brother was fled?

Enter constable [Dogberry, and Verges, with the Watch, leading]
Conrade and Borachio.

195 Dogberry: Come you, sir. If justice cannot tame you, she shall ne'er weigh more reasons in her balance. Nay, an you be a cursing hypocrite once, you must be looked to.

Don Pedro: How now? two of my brother's men bound? Borachio one.

200 Claudio: Hearken after their offence, my lord.

Don Pedro: Officers, what offence have these men done?

Dogberry: Marry, sir, they have committed false report; moreover, they have spoken untruths; secondarily, they are slanders; sixth and lastly, they have belied a lady; thirdly,

205 they have verified unjust things; and to conclude, they are lying knaves.

Don Pedro: First, I ask thee what they have done; thirdly, I ask thee what's their offence; sixth and lastly, why they are committed; and to conclude, what you lay to their

210 charge?

Claudio: Rightly reasoned, and in his own division; and by my troth there's one meaning well suited.

Don Pedro: Who have you offended, masters, that you are thus bound to your answer? This learned constable is too

215 cunning to be understood. What's your offence?

Borachio: Sweet prince, let me go no farther to mine answer. Do you hear me, and let this count kill me. I have deceived even your very eyes. What your wisdoms could not discover, these shallow fools have brought to light,

220 who in the night overheard me confessing to this man, how Don John your brother incensed me to slander the

Lady Hero; how you were brought into the orchard and saw
me court Margaret in Hero's garments; how you disgraced
her when you should marry her. My villainy they have upon
225　　record, which I had rather seal with my death than repeat
over to my shame. The lady is dead upon mine and my master's false accusation; and briefly, I desire nothing but the
reward of a villain.

Don Pedro: Runs not this speech like iron through your blood?

230　Claudio: I have drunk poison whiles he uttered it.

Don Pedro: But did my brother set thee on to this?

Borachio: Yea, and paid me richly for the practice of it.

Don Pedro: He is composed and framed of treachery,
　　And fled he is upon this villainy.

235　Claudio: Sweet Hero, now thy image doth appear
　　In the rare semblance that I loved it first.

Dogberry: Come, bring away the plaintiffs.[18] By this time our
　　sexton hath reformed[19] Signior Leonato of the matter. And,
　　masters, do not forget to specify, when time and place shall
240　　serve, that I am an ass.

Verges: Here, here comes Master Signior Leonato, and the sexton
　　too.

Enter Leonato, [his brother, Antonio, and the sexton.]]

Leonato: Which is the villain? Let me see his eyes,
　　That, when I note another man like him,
245　　I may avoid him. Which of these is he?

Borachio: If you would know your wronger, look on me.

Leonato: Art thou the slave that with thy breath hast killed
　　Mine innocent child?

Borachio: Yea, even I alone.

250　Leonato: No, not so, villain! thou beliest thyself.
　　Here stand a pair of honourable men—
　　A third is fled—that had a hand in it.
　　I thank you princes for my daughter's death.
　　Record it with your high and worthy deeds.
255　　'Twas bravely done, if you bethink you of it.

Claudio: I know not how to pray your patience;
　　Yet I must speak. Choose your revenge yourself;
　　Impose me to what penance your invention
　　Can lay upon my sin. Yet sinned I not
260　　But in mistaking.

[18]*a mistake for
"defendants"*

[19]*informed*

DON PEDRO: By my soul, nor I!
    And yet, to satisfy this good old man,
    I would bend under any heavy weight
    That he'll enjoin me to.

265 LEONATO: I cannot bid you bid my daughter live;
    That were impossible; but I pray you both,
    Possess the people in Messina here
    How innocent she died; and if your love
    Can labour aught[20] in sad invention,
270   Hang her an epitaph upon her tomb,
    And sing it to her bones—sing it to-night.
    To-morrow morning come you to my house,
    And since you could not be my son-in-law,
    Be yet my nephew. My brother hath a daughter,
275   Almost the copy of my child that's dead,
    And she alone is heir to both of us.
    Give her the right you should have giv'n her cousin,
    And so dies my revenge.

CLAUDIO: O noble sir!
280   Your over-kindness doth wring tears from me.
    I do embrace your offer; and dispose
    For henceforth of poor Claudio.

LEONATO: To-morrow then I will expect your coming;
    To-night I take my leave. This naughty man
285   Shall face to face be brought to Margaret,
    Who I believe was packed in all this wrong,
    Hired to it by your brother.

BORACHIO: No, by my soul, she was not;
    Nor knew not what she did when she spoke to me;
290   But always hath been just and virtuous
    In anything that I do know by her.

DOGBERRY: Moreover, my lord, which indeed is not under white and black, this plaintiff here, the offender, did call me ass. I beseech you let it be remembered in his
295 punishment. And also the watch heard them talk of one Deformed. They say he wears a key in his ear, and a lock hanging by it, and borrows money in God's name, the which he hath used so long and never paid that now men grow hard-hearted and will lend nothing for God's sake.
300 Pray you examine him upon that point.

LEONATO: I thank thee for thy care and honest pains.

DOGBERRY: Your worship speaks like a most thankful and reverent youth, and I praise God for you.

[20] any

LEONATO: There's for thy pains. *[Gives money.]*

305 DOGBERRY: God save the foundation!

LEONATO: Go, I discharge thee of thy prisoner, and I thank thee.

DOGBERRY: I leave an arrant knave with your worship, which I
    beseech your worship to correct yourself, for the example
310   of others. God keep your worship! I wish your worship
    well. God restore you to health! I humbly give you leave[21]
    to depart; and if a merry meeting may be wished, God
    prohibit[22] it! Come neighbour.

                            Exeunt [Dogberry and Verges.]

LEONATO: Until to-morrow morning, lords, farewell.

315 ANTONIO: Farewell, my lords. We look for you to-morrow.

DON PEDRO: We will not fail.

CLAUDIO: To-night I'll mourn with Hero.

LEONATO: *[To the Watch]*

    Bring you these fellows on.–We'll talk with Margaret,
320   How her acquaintance grew with this lewd fellow.

                              Exeunt.

SCENE II
[Leonato's Garden]

Enter Benedick and Margaret.

BENEDICK: Pray thee, sweet Mistress Margaret, deserve well at my
    hands by helping me to the speech of Beatrice.

MARGARET: Will you then write me a sonnet in praise of my
    beauty?

5 BENEDICK: In so high a style, Margaret, that no man living shall
    come over[23] it; for in most comely truth thou deservest it.

MARGARET: To have no man come over me? Why, shall I always
    keep below stairs?[24]

BENEDICK: Thy wit is as quick as the greyhound's mouth—it
10   catches.

MARGARET: And yours as blunt as the fencer's foils, which hit but
    hurt not.

BENEDICK: A most manly wit, Margaret; it will not hurt a woman.
    And so I pray thee call Beatrice. I give thee the bucklers.[25]

15 MARGARET: Give us the swords; we have bucklers of our own.

BENEDICK: If you use them, Margaret, you must put in the pikes[26]
    with a vice,[27] and they are dangerous weapons for maids.

[21]*ask your leave*

[22]*permit*

[23]*outdo; Margaret turns the phrase into a sexual pun.*

[24]*i.e., stay down-stairs with the servants*

[25]*shields*

[26]*spikes*

[27]*screw*

MARGARET: Well, I will call Beatrice to you, who I think hath
legs.

20   BENEDICK: And therefore will come.   *Exit Margaret.*

[*Sings*]   The god of love,
             That sits above
             And knows me, and knows me,
             How pitiful I deserve—

25   I mean in singing; but in loving, Leander[28] the good
swimmer, Troilus[29] the first employer of panders,[30] and
a whole book full of these quondam[31] carpet-mongers,[32]
whose names yet run smoothly in the even road of a
blank verse—why, they were never so truly turned over
30   and over as my poor self in love. Marry, I cannot show it
in rhyme. I have tried. I can find out no rhyme to 'lady'
but 'baby'—an innocent rhyme; for 'scorn,' 'horn'—a
hard rhyme; for 'school', 'fool'—a babbling rhyme: very
ominous endings! No, I was not born under a rhyming
35   planet, nor cannot woo in festival[33] terms.

Enter Beatrice.

Sweet Beatrice, wouldst thou come when I called thee?

BEATRICE: Yea, signior, and depart when you bid me.

BENEDICK: O, stay but till then!

BEATRICE: 'Then' is spoken. Fare you well now. And yet, ere I
40   go, let me go with that I came for, which is, with knowing
what hath passed between you and Claudio.

BENEDICK: Only foul words; and thereupon I will kiss thee.

BEATRICE: Foul words is but foul wind, and foul wind is but
foul breath, and foul breath is noisome. Therefore I will
45   depart unkissed.

BENEDICK: Thou hast frighted the word out of his right sense,
so forcible is thy wit. But I must tell thee plainly, Claudio
undergoes my challenge; and either I must shortly hear
from him or I will subscribe him a coward. And I pray
50   thee now tell me, for which of my bad parts didst thou
first fall in love with me?

BEATRICE: For them all together, which maintained so politic[34]
a state of evil that they will not admit any good part to
intermingle with them. But for which of my good parts
55   did you first suffer love for me?

BENEDICK: Suffer love!—a good epithet. I do suffer love
indeed, for I love thee against my will.

---

[28] *a mythical Greek lover (see glossary)*

[29] *a lover in the story of Troilus and Cressida (see glossary)*

[30] *Pandarus. Troilus' uncle, helped him carry messages to Cressida.*

[31] *former*

[32] *false lovers*

[33] *joyful*

[34] *clever*

BEATRICE: In spite of your heart, I think. Alas, poor heart! If you
spite it for my sake, I will spite it for yours, for I will never
60   love that which my friend hates.
BENEDICK: Thou and I are too wise to woo peaceably.
BEATRICE: It appears not in this confession. There's not one wise
man among twenty, that will praise himself.
BENEDICK: An old, an old instance, Beatrice, that lived in the time
65   of good neighbours. If a man do not erect in this age his own
tomb ere he dies, he shall live no longer in monument than
the bell rings and the widow weeps.
BEATRICE: And how long is that, think you?
BENEDICK: Question: why, an hour in clamour and a quarter in
70   rheum.[35] Therefore is it most expedient for the wise, if Don
Worm, his conscience, find no impediment to the contrary,
to be the trumpet of his own virtues, as I am to myself. So
much for praising myself, who, I myself will bear witness,
is praiseworthy. And now tell me, how doth your cousin?
75 BEATRICE: Very ill.
BENEDICK: And how do you?
BEATRICE: Very ill too.

Enter Ursula.

BENEDICK: Serve God, love me, and mend. There will I leave you
too, for here comes one in haste.
80 URSULA: Madam, you must come to your uncle. Yonder's old
coil at home. It is proved my Lady Hero hath been falsely
accused the prince and Claudio mightily abused, and Don
John is the author of all, who is fled and gone. Will you
come presently?
85 BEATRICE: Will you go hear this news, signior?
BENEDICK: I will live in thy heart, die in thy lap, and be buried in
thy eyes; and moreover, I will go with thee to thy uncle's.

Exeunt.

[35]*tears*

SCENE III
[The Inside of a Church]

Enter Claudio, Prince [Don Pedro], and three or four with tapers.

CLAUDIO: Is this the monument of Leonato?
LORD: It is, my lord.
CLAUDIO: *[Reads from a scroll]*

> Epitaph.

5   Done to death by slanderous tongues
       Was the Hero that here lies.
       Death, in guerdon[36] of her wrongs,
       Gives her fame which never dies.
       So the life that died with shame
10   Lives in death with glorious fame.

       [Hanging up the scroll.]
       Hang thou there upon the tomb,
       Praising her when I am dumb.
Now, music, sound, and sing your solemn hymn.
[Song.]

                 Pardon, goddess of the night,[37]
15   Those that slew thy virgin knight;
                 For the which, with songs of woe,
                 Round about her tomb they go.
                 Midnight, assist our moan,
                 Help us to sigh and groan
20   Heavily, heavily,
                 Graves, yawn and yield your dead,
                 Till death be uttered
                 Heavily, heavily.

CLAUDIO: Now unto thy bones good night!
25   Yearly will I do this rite.
DON PEDRO: Good morrow, masters. Put your torches out.
       The wolves have preyed, and look, the gentle day,
       Before the wheels of Phoebus,[38] round about
       Dapples the drowsy east with spots of grey.
30   Thanks to you all, and leave us. Fare you well.
CLAUDIO: Good morrow, masters. Each his several way.
DON PEDRO: Come, let us hence and put on other weeds,[39]
       And then to Leonato's we will go.

---

[36]*reward*

[37]*Diana*

[38]*the sun-god*

[39]*clothing*

CLAUDIO: And Hymen⁴⁰ now with luckier issue speeds
    Than this for whom we rendered up this woe.

⁴⁰the goddess of marriage

                [Exeunt.]

SCENE IV
[A Room in Leonato's House]

Enter Leonato, Benedick, [Beatrice], Margaret, Ursula, [Antonio],
Friar [Francis and] Hero.

FRIAR: Did I not tell you she was innocent?
LEONATO: So are the prince and Claudio, who accused her
    Upon the error that you heard debated.
    But Margaret was in some fault for this,
5   Although against her will, as it appears
    In the true course of all the question.
ANTONIO: Well, I am glad that all things sort so well.
BENEDICK: And so am I, being else by faith enforced
    To call young Claudio to a reckoning for it.
10 LEONATO: Well, daughter, and you gentlewomen all,
    Withdraw into a chamber by yourselves,
    And when I send for you, come hither masked.
    The prince and Claudio promised by this hour
    To visit me. You know your office, brother:
15   You must be father to your brother's daughter,
    And give her to young Claudio.   *Exeunt Ladies.*
ANTONIO: Which I will do with confirmed⁴¹ countenance.⁴²

⁴¹firm
⁴²facial expression

BENEDICK: Friar, I must entreat your pains, I think.
FRIAR: To do what, signior?
20 BENEDICK: To bind me, or undo me—one of them.
    Signior Leonato, truth it is, good signior,
    Your niece regards me with an eye of favour.
LEONATO: That eye my daughter lent her. 'Tis most true.
BENEDICK: And I do with an eye of love requite her.
25 LEONATO: The sight whereof I think you had from me,
    From Claudio, and the prince; but what's your will?
BENEDICK: Your answer, my lord, is enigmatical;
    But, for my will, my will is, your good will
    May stand with ours, this day to be conjoined

30   In the state of honourable marriage;
       In which, good friar, I shall desire your help.
LEONATO: My heart is with your liking.
FRIAR: And my help. Here comes the prince and Claudio.

Enter Prince [Don Pedro] and Claudio with attendants.
DON PEDRO: Good morrow to this fair assembly.
35   LEONATO: Good morrow, prince; good morrow, Claudio.
       We here attend you. Are you yet determined
       To-day to marry with my brother's daughter?
CLAUDIO: I'll hold my mind, were she an Ethiope.
LEONATO: Call her forth, brother. Here's the friar ready.
                            [Exit Antonio.]
40   DON PEDRO: Good morrow, Benedick. Why, what's the matter
       That you have such a February face,
       So full of frost, of storm, and cloudiness?
CLAUDIO: I think he thinks upon the savage bull.
       Tush, fear not, man! We'll tip thy horns with gold,
45   And all Europa shall rejoice at thee,
       As once Europa[43] did at lusty Jove
       When he would play the noble beast in love.
BENEDICK: Bull Jove, my lord, had an amiable low,[44]
       And some such strange bull leaped your father's cow
50   And got a calf in that same noble feat.
       Much like to you, for you have just his bleat.
CLAUDIO: For this I owe you.

Enter [Leonato's] brother, [Antonio], Hero, Beatrice, Margaret,
Ursula, [the ladies wearing masks].
       Here comes other reckonings. Which is the lady I must
       seize upon?
55   ANTONIO: This same is she, and I do give you her.
CLAUDIO: Why then, she's mine. Sweet, let me see your face.
LEONATO: No, that you shall not till you take her hand
       Before this friar and swear to marry her.
CLAUDIO: Give me your hand before this holy friar. I am your
60   husband if you like of me.
HERO: And when I lived I was your other wife; *[Unmasks.]*
       And when you loved you were my other husband.
CLAUDIO: Another Hero!
HERO: Nothing certainer.
65   One Hero died defiled; but I do live,

[43]*a young woman wooed by Jove*

[44]*mooing*

And surely as I live, I am a maid.

DON PEDRO: The former Hero! Hero that is dead!

LEONATO: She died, my lord, but whiles her slander lived.

FRIAR: All this amazement can I qualify,

70   When, after that the holy rites are ended,
I'll tell you largely of fair Hero's death.
Meantime let wonder seem familiar,
And to the chapel let us presently.

BENEDICK: Soft and fair, friar. Which is Beatrice?

75 BEATRICE: *[Unmasks]* I answer to that name. What is your will?

BENEDICK: Do not you love me?

BEATRICE: Why, no; no more than reason.

BENEDICK: Why, then your uncle, and the prince, and Claudio
Have been deceived; for they swore you did.

80 BEATRICE: Do not you love me?

BENEDICK: Troth, no; no more than reason.

BEATRICE: Why, then my cousin, Margaret, and Ursula Are much
deceived; for they did swear you did.

BENEDICK: They swore that you were almost sick for me.

85 BEATRICE: They swore that you were well-nigh dead for me.

BENEDICK: 'Tis no such matter. Then you do not love me?

BEATRICE: No, truly, but in friendly recompense.

LEONATO: Come, cousin, I am sure you love the gentleman.

CLAUDIO: And I'll be sworn upon't that he loves her;

90   For here's a paper written in his hand,
A halting sonnet of his own pure brain,
Fashioned to Beatrice.

HERO: And here's another,
Writ in my cousin's hand, stolen from her pocket,

95   Containing her affection unto Benedick.

BENEDICK: A miracle! Here's our own hands against our hearts.
Come, I will have thee; but, by this light, I take thee for pity.

BEATRICE: I would not deny you; but, by this good day, I yield
upon great persuasion, and partly to save your life, for I was

100   told you were in a consumption.

BENEDICK: Peace! I will stop your mouth. *[Kisses her.]*

DON PEDRO: How dost thou, Benedick, the married man?

BENEDICK: I'll tell thee what, prince; a college of wit-crackers cannot flout me out of my humour. Dost thou think I care for

105   a satire or an epigram?[45] No. If a man will be beaten with
brains, 'a shall wear nothing handsome about him. In brief,
since I do purpose to marry, I will think nothing to any

[45]*formal witticisms*

purpose that the world can say against it; and therefore never flout at me for what I have said against it; for man

110   is a giddy thing, and this is my conclusion. For thy part, Claudio, I did think to have beaten thee; but in that thou art like to be my kinsman, live unbruised, and love my cousin.

CLAUDIO: I had well hoped thou wouldst have denied Beatrice,

115   that I might have cudgelled thee out of thy single life, to make thee a double-dealer, which out of question thou wilt be if my cousin do not look exceeding narrowly to thee.

BENEDICK: Come, come, we are friends. Let's have a dance ere

120   we are married, that we may lighten our own hearts and our wives' heels.

LEONATO: We'll have dancing afterward.

BENEDICK: First, of my word! Therefore play, music. Prince, thou art sad. Get thee a wife, get thee a wife! There is no

125   staff more reverent than one tipped with horn.

Enter Messenger.

MESSENGER: My lord, your brother Don John is taken in flight,
And brought with armed men back to Messina.

BENEDICK: Think not on him till to-morrow. I'll devise thee brave punishments for him. Strike up, pipers!

Dance. [Exeunt.]

Glossary and Vocabulary

Act I, scene i

birdbolt – a beginners' level in archery; Beatrice is mocking both Benedick's boastful nature and his inability to do serious damage both in love and in war.

jade's trick – A *jade* is an unreliable horse, one which might stop in the last stretch of a race. Beatrice accuses Benedick of abruptly and unfairly dropping out of their battle of wits.

play the flouting Jack – tease us; Benedick asks if Claudio is trying to get them to believe that Cupid, usually portrayed as blind, has great vision, or that Vulcan, the famous blacksmith, is actually a great carpenter.

sometime guarded with fragments – In response to Claudio and Pedro's mockery of his speech, Benedick retorts that their wittiness is lacking coherence. Wordplay is very important in *Much Ado About Nothing*; characters are always criticizing, building on, and playing off of each others' words and phrasing. Formal styles of writing and speaking are often referenced (as here, when a casual word becomes the closing of a letter or at the wedding of Claudio and Hero, when Benedick quotes a widely-used Latin grammar phrase).

Act I, scene iii

born under Saturn – During Elizabethan times, most people believed that the positions of the planets played a great role in a person's temperament. Because Don John was born under Saturn, he is supposed to have a gloomy nature.

Act II, scene i

Philemon – A classical myth relates that an elderly husband (Philemon) and his wife (Baucis) invited a stranger into their home. Although they were poor, they gave the guest everything they could; they were rewarded when the guest turned out to be Jove, king of the gods, in disguise. Don Pedro tells Hero that his real face is much more attractive than his mask in the same way that the face of Jove was more attractive than Philemon's roof.

Answer, clerk – Margaret pretends that she and Balthasar are in a formal question-and-answer period similar to the one used in church services; as *clerk*, Balthasar is supposed to supply the responses to Margaret's questions.

Hercules – In Greek and Roman mythology, Hercules was the strongest man in the world. Benedick complains that Beatrice would have reduced even Hercules to the humblest position—that of turning the spit on which a piece of meat was cooking.

Antipodes – places on Earth that are opposite of each other; often, it is a reference to Australia and New Zealand, which are diametrically opposed to England—the other side of the earth.

harpy – Both the Greek author Homer and the Roman author Virgil mention these foul half-women, half-vultures in their long poems. The name *harpy* eventually became synonymous with "bad-tempered woman."

ACT II, SCENE III

orthography – literally, the formal study of spelling; Benedick means that Claudio's language has gone from being plain and straightforward to fancy and formal.

Hector – a Trojan warrior famous for his strength and bravery

ACT III, SCENE I

limed – Lime was a sticky substance that hunters used to catch birds.

ACT III, SCENE II

but a humour or a worm – according to Elizabethan medicine, two possible causes of a toothache; a *humour* is one of four bodily fluids (black bile, yellow bile, phlegm, and blood) that Elizabethans believed determined a person's temperament.

ACT III, SCENE III

suffer salvation – In this and Act III, Scene v, Act IV, Scene ii, and Act V, Scene i, we see Dogberry attempting to use complex and elevated language, with humorous results. His mistakes in this scene are as follows:

- *salvation* for *damnation*
- *allegiance* for *disloyalty*
- *desartless* for *deserving*
- *senseless* for *sensible*
- *comprehend* for *apprehend*
- *vagrom* for *vagrant*
- *tolerable* for *intolerable*
- *bills* for *weapons*
- *present* for *represent*

Bel – Borachio makes a reference to a book from the *Apocrypha* called "Bel and the Dragon." (The *Apocrypha* is a collection of books that some Christians consider Scripture and others believe should be excluded from the Bible). The window portraying Bel (actually the Phoenician god Baal), along with the other pictures that Borachio mentions, gives us an idea of fashion as being somewhat dirty and effeminate.

ACT III, SCENE IV

turned Turk – Margaret says that if Beatrice had not *turned Turk* (that is, gone back on her vow not to love, just as if she had gone back on her Christian vows and become a Muslim), there will be no "sailing by the star"—i.e., if it is not certain that Beatrice is in love, then nothing is certain.

ACT III, SCENE V

decerns – Dogberry makes the following mistakes in this scene:

- *confidence* for *conference*
- *decerns* for *concerns*
- *blunt* for *sharp*
- *odorous* for *odious*
- *tedious* for *something like "wealthy"*

- *exclamation* for *acclamation*
- *comprehended* for *apprehended*
- *aspicious* for *auspicious*
- *suffigance* for *sufficient*
- *examination* for *examine*
- *non-come* for *nonplus*
- *excommunication* for *communication*

Act IV, scene i

catechizing – *Catechism* was a form of religious questioning once used in the Catholic Church. In the older version of a formal *catechism*, a person was asked a series of questions about faith and God, and was instructed to give specific, memorized answers. Hero feels that she is caught in a perversion of the original catechism; the line of questioning that Claudio is pursuing seems designed to prove her guilty rather than display her faith.

Act IV, scene ii

dissembly – In this scene, Dogberry makes the following errors:
- *dissembly* for *assembly*
- *malefactors* for *accusers*
- *perjury* for *treason*
- *redemption* for *damnation*
- *opinioned* for *pinioned*
- *suspect* for *respect*
- *piety* for *impiety*

Act V, scene i

calf's head...capon...woodcock—The three items Claudio mentions are foods that were traditionally served at banquets, but they are also symbolic of negative qualities. *Calf's head* and *woodcock* both mean "fool," while *capon* (a castrated chicken) is another name for a eunuch.

horns – A *cuckold* is a man whose wife cheats on him; the traditional sign of a cuckold is a pair of horns.

Dogberry's mistakes:
- *plaintiffs for defendants*
- *reformed for informed*
- *give you leave for ask your leave*
- *prohibit for permit*

Act V, scene ii

Leander – In the story of Hero and Leander, as told by the Roman poet Ovid, Leander swims nightly across a channel to visit Hero, his mistress.

Troilus – The Middle English poet Chaucer tells the story of Troilus and Cressida, two lovers who employed a courier to deliver their messages to one another. The name of the courier, Pandarus, gives us the English word *pander*.

Insightful and Reader-Friendly, Yet Affordable

Prestwick House Literary Touchstone Classic Editions– The Editions By Which All Others May Be Judged

Every *Prestwick House Literary Touchstone Classic* is enhanced with Reading Pointers for Sharper Insight to improve comprehension and provide insights that will help students recognize key themes, symbols, and plot complexities. In addition, each title includes a Glossary of the more difficult words and concepts.

For the Shakespeare titles, along with the Reading Pointers and Glossary, we include margin notes and various strategies to understanding the language of Shakespeare.

New titles are constantly being added; call or visit our website for current listing.

Special Educator's Discount – At Least

50% Off

		Educator's Retail Price	Discount
200053	**Adventures of Huckleberry Finn**	~~$4.99~~	**$2.49**
202118	**Antigone**	~~$3.99~~	**$1.99**
200141	**Awakening, The**	~~$5.99~~	**$2.99**
200179	**Christmas Carol, A**	~~$3.99~~	**$1.99**
200694	**Doll's House, A**	~~$3.99~~	**$1.99**
200054	**Frankenstein**	~~$4.99~~	**$1.99**
200091	**Hamlet**	~~$3.99~~	**$1.99**
200074	**Heart of Darkness**	~~$3.99~~	**$1.99**
200147	**Importance of Being Earnest, The**	~~$3.99~~	**$1.99**
200146	**Julius Caesar**	~~$3.99~~	**$1.99**
200125	**Macbeth**	~~$3.99~~	**$1.99**
200081	**Midsummer Night's Dream, A**	~~$3.99~~	**$1.99**
200079	**Narrative of the Life of Frederick Douglass**	~~$3.99~~	**$1.99**
200564	**Oedipus Rex**	~~$3.99~~	**$1.99**
200095	**Othello**	~~$3.99~~	**$1.99**
200193	**Romeo and Juliet**	~~$3.99~~	**$0.99**
200132	**Scarlet Letter, The**	~~$5.99~~	**$2.99**
200251	**Tale of Two Cities, A**	~~$6.99~~	**$3.49**

Prestwick House

Prestwick House, Inc. • P.O. Box 658, Clayton, DE 19938
Phone (800) 932-4593 • Fax (888) 718-9333 • www.prestwickhouse.com